the Shoes of Kilimanjaro

and other oddventure travel stories

by
Cameron M. Burns

303/500

Disclaimer: This book is not a guide to adventure travel. The information in this book should not be considered anything more than entertainment, or something sort of resembling entertainment. The author and the publisher of this book do not guarantee results. Additionally, the author and the publisher assume no responsibility for the actions of any person who might try to recreate the situations described in this book.

—The Editors, Hard-Pressed Books

The Shoes of Kilimanjaro

And Other Oddventure Travel Stories

By Cameron M. Burns

Hard-Pressed Books
P.O. Box 1925
Basalt, CO 81621
USA

Published by
Hard-Pressed Books
P.O. Box 1925
Basalt, CO 81621

First edition, January 2002

Manufactured in the United States of America

Edited by a collection of shaggy people in my living room
Book design by Cameron M. Burns
Cover painting ("The Shoes of Kili," 11X17" watercolor on paper) by Cameron M. Burns. All artwork by Cameron M. Burns
Author photo © 2001 by Norm Clasen

Library of Congress Cataloging-In-Publication Data
Burns, Cameron M.
The Shoes of Kilimanjaro & Other Oddventure Travel Stories/Cameron M. Burns

ISBN: 0-9629627-1-6

This book is set in Times, with Crazy Harold titles, a Dominican disclaimer, and Pharmacy company name. The cover font is called "Shoes of Kili," designed by Cameron M. Burns

For Bob and Sylvia

Contents

Introduction: What is Oddventure? 9

In the Mountains

The Shoes of Kilimanjaro 15
In Patagonian Therapy 23
Touching the 'Roid 31

Across Great Oceans

The Sydney-to-Hobart Race 47
Inbreds in the Stream 55

The Animal Kingdom

Perro Café 77
I Dreamed of African Lions 89
The Arachnids of Arenal 105
Bathtubs Along the Ewaso Ngiro 113

On the *Road*

Holy Cows and Traffic Jams 131
Dribbling the Elks 141
Out of the Box in Hong Kong 149
Round about Wales 163

Notes on the Essays 175

Acknowledgements

There are a handful of superbly talented editors out there who helped whip these stories into shape for their inclusion in various publications, and without their help I would have never thought them worth printing: Carrie Click, John Colson, Scott Condon, Donna Dowling, Kisha Ferguson, Stephen Fisher, Sara Garton, Aaron Gulley, Claire Hochachka, Dougald MacDonald, Stewart Oksenhorn, Tom Prentice, Amy Schrier, Hilary White and, last but not least, Andy Stone.

Thanks to all my family members who enjoyed part of this weird trip called life: Mary and Kerry Burns; Penny, Michael, Jessica, Natalie and Katie Sandy; Gillian, Glenn, Ryan and Kelsea Haste; and Johnny, Myra, Beau, Desha and Joel Bone.

Thanks also to Pete Athans, Laurie Bower, Jon and Holly Butler, John, Jenny, Sophie and Ian Catto, Bryan Gall, Leslie Henderson, Rob Hering, Loren and Missy Jenkins, Luke and Mel Laeser, Paul "Beaver" McBride, Chris and Courtney Pomeroy, Steve, Sandy, Tori and Angelo Porcella, Margaret and Paula Quenemoen, Mike, Claire, Liam and Nicole Schillaci, Ed Webster, Jeff, Dawn and Sienna Widen.

Thanks also to my friends at Rocky Mountain Institute: Amory Lovins, Hunter Lovins, Marty Pickett, Tom Feiler, David Elliot, Randi Lowenthal, Karl Rábago, Bill Browning, Jason Denner, Huston Eubank, Peter Gage, Catherine Greener, Rick Heede, Joanie Henderson, Christopher Juniper, Alexis Karolides, Michael Kinsley, Chris Lotspeich, Christina Page, Kate Parrot, David Payne, Richard Pinkham, Jeremy Magliaro, Ben Shepherd, Joel Swisher, Bob Wilkinson, Dale Levy, Stephanie Gilchrist, Charmaine Boudreaux, Nancy Johnston, Norm Clasen, Jenny Constable, Brian Adams, Ben Emerson, Thammy Evans, Jeremy Heiman, Christopher Juniper, Ruth Klock, Peter Light, Jill Randall, Dave Reed, Bill Simon, Steve Swanson, Trish Chew, Patsy Hernandez, Marty Hagen, Todd Kline, Paul Buch, Amanda Ayres, Eliza Eubank, Ethel Lossing, John Anderson, Red Cain, Melissa Newsom, John Roberts, Doreen Clavell, Lori Klein, Kortney Hartman, Jennifer Sweeting, Sunny Harrison, Missy Morgan, Michelle Sandoval, Marilyn Wien, and the late, great Farley Sheldon.

I am grateful for the help of the following companies, who kindly donated the finest equipment so that I might try to destroy it during some of these trips: Jagged Edge Mountain Gear (Margaret and Paula Quenemoen), Outdoor Research (Jim Meyers), Gregory Mountain Products (Paul Gagner, Dion Goldsworthy), The North Face (Jill Pagliaro, Jason Oelkers), Mountain Safety Research (Todd Benevedos), Leki, Cascade Designs (Tommy Myers), Solomon, Asolo (Stu Coulter), Jibs, and Petzl. Lufthansa (Jim Freeman) helped my wife and me get to East Africa cheaply—thanks.

Chris McBride and Bill Bryson provided encouragement, and Australia's greatest artist, Norman Lindsay, provided inspiration.

What is Oddventure?

What is *Oddventure*? Well, put simply, it's a term I came up with years ago when a friend asked about some of my travel writing. Since then, I've learned it is—apparently—fairly common. So much for original ideas.

Anyway, my friend didn't quite understand how I'd come up with some of my angles for articles on fairly pedestrian topics. Being a newspaperman for much of my obviously short adult life, I explained that in the news reporting business, reporters are often required to put fresh perspectives on tired old topics—the dreaded spin. Oddventure, I explained, was my spin on the standard old travel topics that have been beaten to death by every travel and adventure writer on the face of the planet.

But before I explain oddventure any further, it's important to first ask: what is adventure? That's an even better question, and with every passing year, a lot of daring souls try to answer it, either through dramatic action or in dramatic words. Often both. Of course, having grown up as a climber, adventure has meant a new climbing game with nearly every season: new gear, new techniques, new crags, a new big wall area, a new mountain range to be explored and conquered.

In other sports, adventure has seen a similar evolution. The latest rage in skiing is extreme skiing, not just in back bowls of your local hills, but down sheer mountain faces in Alaska. The latest ocean sport is surfing monster waves that require being towed by a Jet Ski in order to get started. Parasailers are currently pushing the heights at which they fly, soaring to levels where oxygen is required.

There are two definitions that most of us from the latter 20th century/early 21st century agree upon when it comes to adventure. The first is that we generally think of adventure as having to be outdoors, preferably in a wilderness setting. The more remote, the greater the adventure. The other thing about adventure is that we generally associate it with an activity that can be life-threatening, where someone has the potential to be seriously injured or die. The more life-threatening, the greater the adventure.

Webster's New World Dictionary of the American Language [1962 edition] defines it in about five different ways, most of which center around taking risks, i.e., "1. the encountering of danger," and "2. an exciting and dangerous undertaking, etc."

Not once in Noah Webster's great tome does the definition mention wilderness or remote settings. Furthermore, danger is defined as "a thing that may cause injury, pain, etc." The word doesn't necessarily mean someone might die. In other words, for many of us, our 21st century version of adventure—death-defying outdoor activities—is our own projection of what adventure really means. I'm not quite sure who's to blame, if anyone. Certainly, many masters of these sports deem the accomplishments of the masses less than cutting-edge. The superstar surfer who now teaches the sport might find riding the waves of a ten-year storm boring. The accomplished skier who has conquered Alaskan mountain faces might see a five-day ski traverse close to home as mundane.

But then, consider the abilities of these people. The highly trained mountaineer who is attempting a new route on a remote peak in Patagonia, for example, will likely use no technique that is new to him, will have the route mapped out in his mind before he begins, will know the descent route he plans to take. About the only uncertainty, in Patagonia anyway, is the weather.

And because those of us pursuing activities at a grade or rating below these masters admire those masters and covet their experience and ability, we are put into a frame of mind that what we're doing isn't really an adventure, just an everyday activity within that branch of the sport. We are told that true adventure takes one heck of a lot of experience, is incredibly death-defying, and that it can't be found close to home.

I submit that adventure need not involve wilderness or death-defying activities, but is centered wholly on doing something new. Adventure can be much more subtle—as subtle as a traveling somewhere you've never been, trying a new hobby, learning a new language. Some of the most adventurous moments of my life have been cleaning out my outdoor storage locker where I keep my skis, climbing equipment and outdoor gear. It's full of all sorts of weird, wonderful and scary critters.

Adventure, I believe, should focus more on Webster's third definition: "an unusual, stirring experience, often of romantic nature."

For me adventure also means a challenge to human sensibilities. Can you laugh in the face of adversity? Can you deal with other humans who don't understand your beliefs, customs or language? Can you make fun of your own situation? Or will you simply give up and go home?

Some of the oddventures in this book were created by chance. Some of them were created, at least partly, by my own deviant mind. All of them live up to Webster's third explanation ("an unusual, stirring experience, often of romantic nature").

My March 1997 camel safari in Northern Kenya (see "Bathtubs Along the Ewaso Ngiro") figured as one of the former. It was a luxury trip designed for tourists: well-stocked camps, vehicular support, professional guides and cooks, and all the creature comforts of home. But as the week-long trip progressed, and we found ourselves encountering more and more bizarre mishaps, our adventure became a test of our collective sense of humor. In the end we dealt with all the problems and came away with the experience of a lifetime, an experience far greater than bland memories of a trip where everything had gone smoothly. "Dribbling the Elks," however, was an oddventure I conjured up, then attempted to execute. That, too, was a disaster in the sense of trying to meet a challenge. But as all journeys do, it offered many other meaningful moments: the chance to take a unique trip with a close friend, the chance to explore wilderness in my back yard, the chance simply to be outside.

Each of the stories in this collection is about some unique place and some unique experience. Originally, they were written for a broad mixture of publications: mountaineering magazines and adventure journals, newspapers and travel anthologies. Generally, the essays are unrelated and were written years, even decades apart. The common thread that runs through these oddventuers is just how odd they were.

I hope you enjoy them and regard your travels, your experiences, and your everyday life as nothing short of a joyous and hilarious phenomenon. Nothing beats a good laugh. More importantly, I hope you remember to laugh the next time you get a flat tire in Africa, have a starving dog whimper for food in Mexico, or wonder whether you're ready for a leisurely sailing trip.

IN THE MOUNTAINS

The Shoes of Kilimanjaro

(Tanzania, 1997)

"There, ahead, all he could see, as wide as all the world, great, high, and unbelievably white in the sun, was the square top of Kilimanjaro."

—Ernest Hemingway, *The Snows of Kilimanjaro*

If you ever get to the foot of Kilimanjaro in East Africa, there are two sights that will take your breath away. First there's the mountain itself. The looming hulk of this huge, seemingly out-of-place extinct volcano hovers above the East African plain like a gigantic, otherworldly spacecraft, quietly poised to nab hundreds of unsuspecting humans for exotic experiments on the far side of the Universe. The second sight that will take your breath away—and leave you simultaneously gasping in awe and scratching your head—are the shoes worn by the locals. That's right, the shoes.

I'm not talking about just any local, however, as there are tens of thousands of friendly Tanzanians inhabiting the towns, villages and farmlands surrounding Kilimanjaro who seem to have a fairly normal range of footwear for a dry, dusty ecotone sitting astride the equator. I'm talking about the shoes worn by the porters and guides on the mountain. They are, to put it mildly, one of the most astonishing things you will ever see.

My odd relationship with Kilimanjaro's shoes began in late 1996, when I landed a job to write a climbing guide for an American publishing company about climbing the mountain. My wife Ann was to accompany me on the trip, and, sometime around October, we began planning our mini-expedition.

Although, Kilimanjaro requires little more than some steep hiking by its most popular routes, we took our planning seriously, as if we were mounting an assault on K2, Fitzroy or Mt. McKinley. We started out by making lists because, after all, lists keep you organized. Or at least make you think you're organized. We had lists of things to do, lists of people to call, lists of arrangements to make with bill collectors, lists of diseases you can catch. We also made endless lists of gear to bring: tents, warm clothes, gear, accessories.

Nearly every item on our gear list was a simple matter of yes or no. Yes we need it; no, we don't. But things got awfully fuzzy when it came to footwear. Would river-rafting sandals or sneakers be better in the hot, dry towns we'd travel through? Would sneakers be adequate for walking through the jungles on the lower part of the mountain? Would I need plastic mountaineering boots at the top, or would leather boots suffice?

In the end, after much profound soul-searching, I packed some sandals, a pair of sneakers, a pair of high-topped canvas boots, and a pair of midweight leather mountaineering boots. I also threw in a pair of down booties, for around camp and in the tent. Six pairs altogether. Once my pile of footgear was combined with Ann's flotilla of sandals, boots and athletic shoes, we had 12 pairs—24 individual shoes all told, enough to fill one of our duffel bags entirely. Enough to make Imelda Marcos nervous.

At the airport, we paid $50 for our extra baggage (i.e. shoes), and once we landed in Nairobi, my wife and I found we had to tip taxi drivers and tour operators extra because we had so much stuff.

On January 2, we began the first of six routes we would climb on the mountain. A rented Land Rover dumped Ann and me, along with our required guide and four porters, at the Kilimanjaro National Park gate, and after the porters had organized their loads, we started walking through the montane forests that occupy Kilimanjaro's lower slopes. I was in my sandals; Ann was in her walking shoes.

Our guide William wore a pair of Adiddas sneakers, at least six sizes too big and looking remarkably like clown shoes. I later learned they had been donated by a German tourist. They looked like knockoffs—you know, cheap shoes manufactured illegally in China or Indonesia but made to look like the real thing. William couldn't have cared less—his clown shoes were a status symbol. Meanwhile, our porters—Michael, Alan, Mohammed and John—wore beach thongs. Beach thongs!? I did a double take and stared at the dusty, cracked brown heels in front of me. Wow! Are these guys nuts? I watched the clip-clapping shoes as I followed Michael through the forest. This took awhile to get used to: beach thongs on a mountain nearly 6,000 meters tall.

Regardless of the state of their footwear, none of the porters—or William, for that matter—seemed the least bit handicapped by their footwear. Indeed, while Michael deftly maneuvered over slick, wet tree roots with the precision of a ballerina, Ann and I tripped over every log. When John nimbly tiptoed around and over sections of bog, we stumbled straight through, the mud up to our ankles. While Alan danced up short cliff bands encountered along the trail, we quavered in fright on the crumbling hand and footholds. And as Mohammed sped along the rough gravel slopes below the southern glaciers, we skidded and fell, unsure of ourselves on the rhyolite gravel. Not only did Michael, Alan, Mohammed and John do all this with 70 pounds on their backs, (Ann and I had day packs that might as well have been filled with Styrofoam peanuts) we were cheating by using trekking poles for balance.

That evening, when we reached the first of four camps we'd make on Kili, I exchanged my sandals for my camp booties and Ann put on some lightweight hiking boots. The next morning, I switched to sneakers, and Ann put on her walking shoes again.

As the days drifted by and we crept ever higher on the mountain, Ann and I changed shoes every half day or so. Sneakers to canvas boots. Canvas boots to walking shoes. Sneakers to leather mountaineering boots. Leather mountaineering boots to canvas boots, and so on—a foot fetish equal to the best of perversions. As we fussed over our feet, our Tanzanian friends—in their beach thongs—watched in amusement. We were obviously appeasing some strange Western deity who had bestowed our weird religion with meticulous rules regarding feet.

On January 4, we reached the highest camp on the mountain, and the porters finally changed their footgear. Michael put on a pair of brown leather penny loafers. The seams were split and re-sewn with white string and the soles looked slick as ice. Alan and Mohammed both put on pairs of ripped sneakers. The treads were more suited to a grassy football field or a basketball court than a rocky trail. Meanwhile, John put on a pair of worn leather wingtips, the kind a bum in New York City's old Bowery might wear. (And, come to think of it,

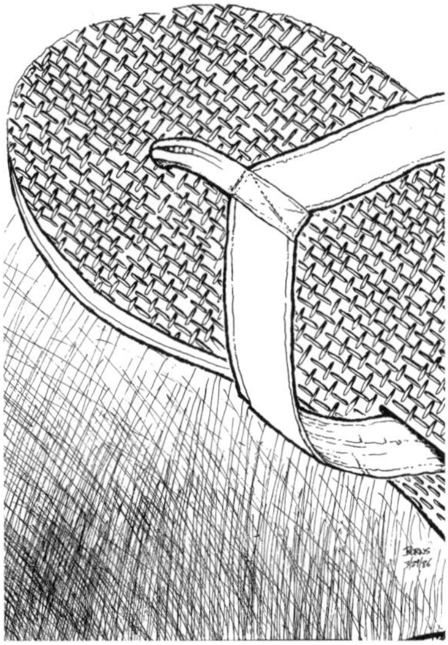

John looked like he belonged in the old Bowery.) We sat around a small fire that night, the night before our final day of the climb, eating, laughing and sipping mugs of tea. Secretly, we were regarding each other's feet.

In all the world's societies, shoes are an important symbol of wealth and class. Imelda, the wife of the late Filipino ruler Ferdinand Marcos, acquired some 3,000 pairs of shoes while her husband was in power. Her status as one of the wealthiest women in the world was justified, in part, by her shoes. The famous children's fairy tale, *Cinderella*, tells of a poor cinder maid who shoots straight to queenhood after her foot is found to fit a glass slipper that a charming prince is toting around the countryside while searching for an appropriately sized foot.

But shoes are more than symbols of status. They are icons of change, improvement and escape. Since the beginning of human evolution, shoes have represented mobility. By using their feet (and thus their shoes) ancient human races were able to run away from saber-toothed tigers and advancing ice sheets. Nomadic peoples could migrate in search of water and game. Shoes represented the ability to get out of a bad situation and, hopefully, into a better one. Shoes allow us to change our circumstances, the circumstances of our progeny and the circumstances of entire civilizations, so for thousands of years they have been given special, sometimes magical attributes.

"Throughout history footwear has figured widely in mythology, folk stories and superstition," wrote shoe aficionado Richard N. DeCost, a professional shoemaker from Massachusetts—obviously a guy as nutty about footwear as myself. "The Greek god Mercury wore winged sandals, and there are very few Europeans who do not remember childhood tales of 'Puss in Boots,' the 'Seven League Boots,' 'Cinderella' and 'The Old Woman Who Lived in a Shoe,' and most cultures have stories where shoes play a starring role."

Ponder L. Frank Baum's book *The Wonderful Wizard of Oz* for a moment. This book is often described as a fairy tale, but it's actually a story about shoes. Much of the plot details the Wicked Witch of the West's quest for Dorothy's silver shoes, which hold immense magical power. (Incidentally, the shoes started out belonging to the Wicked Witch of the West's sister, the Wicked Witch of the East, but were taken by Dorothy after Dorothy's house flattened the Eastern-dwelling sorceress.) In 1939, Metro-Goldwyn-Mayer screenwriter Noel Langley decided that for the film based on the book, Dorothy's silver shoes would be red slippers. Today, Langley's version of the shoes, those ruby slippers, is an international icon.

As we all remember, it's the ruby slippers that hold the power to correct all Dorothy's problems—namely, get her back home to Kansas. "There's no place like home" is one of the most-quoted lines of movie script anywhere in history, and it's all centered around Dorothy's red pumps and their magical powers. (Incidentally, on May 24, 2000, Hollywood movie memorabilia collector David Elkouby paid $600,000 for the shoes worn by Judy Garland in the film version, *The Wizard of Oz*, at a Hollywood memorabilia auction in New York City.)

Shoes are more than icons of change. They're symbols of power, good luck and control. Think of all the songs that have been written about shoes. Nancy Sinatra's "These Boots Were Made for Walking" told of her ability to walk out on a man as well as to "walk all over" him, equating boots to a powerful weapon of revenge. Elvis Presley's "Blue Suede Shoes" told the story of a man who would let another fellow "knock me down, step on my face, slander my name all over the place … burn my house, steal my car, drink my liquor from my old fruit jar ...." Pretty much anything was okay, just as long as the antagonist did not "step on my blue suede shoes."

Shoes have even changed our language. Consider the following ideas and expressions: "give him the boot," "on a shoestring," "fill one's shoes," "put yourself in my shoes," "the shoe is on the other foot now," "goody two-shoes," "bet your boots," "die with your boots on," "lick his boots," "pull yourself up by your bootstraps," "walk a mile in my shoes," "heart in your shoes," "well-heeled," and "put on your dancin' shoes."

Ruth Tanenhous, author of *The Great American Foot* wrote that "in an average lifetime, our feet carry us over 65,000 miles, more than two and a half times around the world," so why wouldn't we consider our shoes important?

Indeed, a web page that no longer exists used to list Emma Peel's boots as the most important attraction at the Planet Hollywood restaurant in Las Vegas. Who was Emma Peel, you ask? She was the saucy, martial arts-kicking female do-gooder of *The Avengers'* fame—but that doesn't really matter. What matters is that her shoes were cited ahead of James Bond's trick car devices and Theda Bara's headdress in a description of Las Vegas museums on the Internet.

Anyway, you get my point. Shoes are pretty darn important. They get us out of trouble, they carry us off to better places, they let us see new horizons and they allow us to know our world. And they accessorize with everything!

In the morning—if 1 a.m. counts as morning—Ann, William and I arose, and toiled up five kilometers of frozen gravel to the summit of Kilimanjaro, where, predictably, we ran smack into a crowd, all milling about in the dawn light and celebrating their few minutes of glory on top of Africa. Three German tourists wearing huge, neon-green Koflach plastic mountaineering boots stood side-by-side with local guides wearing leather street shoes. A British couple, in $200-a-pair leather hiking boots and gaiters slapped the backs of a Tanzanian porter—an apprentice guide—who was wearing a pair of lightweight vinyl cross-country skiing shoes. And I hung around with William, in his knockoff Adiddas boats, six sizes too big and now that I really studied them, hideously ugly.

We descended back to camp, packed up and then turned our attention to the descent through the forests. Our mini-expedition was an enormous success, and we were ready to celebrate our incredible, historic achievement—even though we were just three of 70 who summitted that day.

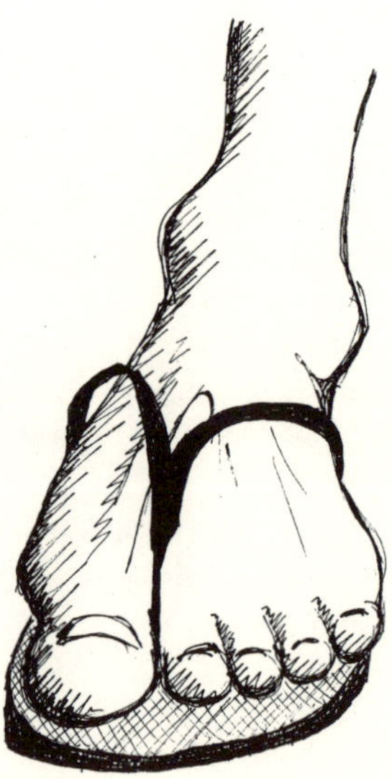

One of the most important aspects about mountain climbing is bragging rights. Mountain climbers dote on their ability to report not only making a summit, but also making it by "fair means," or in a way that is more challenging than the way most other climbers have made the ascent.

In 1968, two one-legged Austrians, Otto Umlauf and Thomas Karcher, who were crippled during World War II, climbed Kilimanjaro. In 1969, seven blind African boys climbed Kili as far as Gillman's Point.[1] In 1994, American climbers Kevin Cooney and John Winsor ran up the Marangu Route, taking seven hours and 11 minutes from the gate to the summit of Kibo, and 12 hours and 45 minutes for the whole trip. And in 1981, Swiss mountaineer Fritz Lortscher reported that he had climbed Kilimanjaro at least 33 times.

But these achievements seem small when one considers that many of the guides and porters from the village of Marangu have not only climbed the mountain over 200 times, they've done it in totally junk footwear. And here, perhaps, is the kicker—they choose to climb the mountain in their crap shoes.

A few days after our first climb up the mountain, Ann and I bumped into Mohammed on the streets of Moshi, the small town sitting at the base of the mountain. He was with a group of fellow locals, all vying for a job portering for the next round of tourists. And, we noticed, Mohammed was wearing very nice, very new hiking boots, a far cry from the beach thongs and crummy sneakers he'd worn on the mountain. We pulled him aside and politely grilled him about his footwear.

"These?" he asked in response to our accusatory fingers. "These are my good shoes. I wouldn't want to take them up on the mountain. I wouldn't want to ruin them. I use my old shoes up there, where it doesn't matter if they get damaged."

Somehow, over the decades, as writers, philosophers, film directors and artists of all genre have waxed eloquent about Kilimanjaro, the shoes have been ignored. Indeed, the most famous of all literary works that mentions Kilimanjaro, "The Snows of Kilimanjaro" by Ernest Hemingway, doesn't once mention anything about footwear. I know—I've skimmed the story twice. As I watched Mohammed walk back across the street to rejoin the group of porters all vying for a week's employment, something similar to what Ernest Hemingway had written 60 years ago came to mind.

"There, ahead, all he could see, as crappy as any product in all the world, tragic, worthless, and unbelievably flimsy on the trail, were the shoes of Kilimanjaro."

1. Gillman's Point is a point located on the crater rim of Kilimanjaro. Although lower than the actual summit, most climbers on the normal route reach Gillman's Point before walking around Kili's crater to the top. Many turn back at Gillman's Point.

In Patagonian Therapy

(Argentina, 1995-96)

"Fresh projects kept occurring to my mind, each more compelling than the last."
—Eric Shipton, *Land of Tempest*

It took me three weeks of sitting in a smelly, dirty tent that looked like the interior of a broken washing machine to learn that mountaineering in Patagonia has little to do with climbing.

To be sure, there are the days when the sky dawns bright and clear and the wind stops howling for a few hours, when you run out and snatch a summit if you're very, very lucky. More than likely, you climb about half a route, then have to retreat in the soggiest, windiest blizzard you can remember, empty-handed. Then you sit and wait a couple of weeks for whatever comes next. Often it's nothing. Patagonia is that way—it has the worst weather on the planet and some of the most beautiful mountains.

Nope, I'm convinced, climbing in Patagonia is about something else. Although everyone's planning to climb something—talking about it, dreaming about it, eating, sleeping, and breathing climbing—not a whole lot of climbing is getting done. In reality, the 100 or so young men that dwell in the beech forests below the world's most spectacular peaks for the four months of the austral summer are simply looking for something to do.

In December 1995, two English climbing buddies, Julian Fisher and Charlie French, and I headed south to Argentine Patagonia for a six-week attempt to climb Cerro Fitzroy. Fitzroy and its neighbor, Cerro Torre, are the two most famous mountains in this far southern area of the Andes, and climbers from all over the world head there to try their luck on the peaks. The mountains are under 12,000 feet tall (paltry, really, compared to our mountains in the western United States), but what they lack in height is more than made up for in technical difficulty. Both peaks combined have been climbed fewer times than Everest.

More onerous than the technical difficulties, however, is the weather. Unhampered by terra firma, winds whip around the lower portions of the Southern Hemisphere with the fury of a hurricane, meaning that in order to climb, you have to wait for a clear day. Sometimes, for months on end. Most climbers end up biding their time in the Rio Blanco camp (below Fitzroy) or the Campo Bridwell (below Cerro Torre), and as Julian, Charlie and I were soon to learn, these basecamps are truly weird places.

When the three of us arrived around mid-December, our first thoughts were that we'd stumbled into a refugee camp. Dozens of scraggly young men, clad in filthy long underwear and sporting patchy beards, moped about a cluster of ruinous shacks that looked like piles of construction debris set amid a beech forest. POW camps, Jonestown, Guyana, and William Golding's classic story *Lord of the Flies* all came to mind at once. I had flashbacks to every Greyhound bus station I'd ever slept in.

It was an anarchic society, a fringe civilization dwelling between the Neanderthal epoch and present day. Scary monobrows and descending hairlines complimented the latest in high technology. Gizmos of all kinds were strapped to the scruffiest of Missing Links. With every patch of blue sky that floated overhead, dozens of wrists would be bared and excited consultations with barometer watches would ensue. Everyone who had a watch—even if the watch's most advanced feature was an alarm—became an instant meteorologist, and speculation on what the weather would do next ran the gamut from full-blown optimism (i.e., packing up gear and strapping on boots) to downright disgust, which was expressed, for the most part, by crawling back into a tent.

All the excited speculation would last only until the next set of white clouds floated overhead. Then everyone would sulk back into the weird daydream of being in a lush wilderness, thousands of miles from home, with no real purpose for the day. (An employment office would do brisk business here.) Thus, you begin to look for one—a purpose that is.

Take Gunnar, a clockmaker from Germany, for example. He spent the first two weeks of his visit to Argentina hauling over 50 pounds of potatoes between the nearby village of Chalten and the Rio Blanco basecamp at the foot of Fitzroy. Certainly hauling 50 pounds of potatoes can be done in a couple of days, but Gunnar felt the task needed his full attention for about 14. On several clear mornings, as Julian, Charlie and I humped gear and food to Paso Superior for a night in a snow cave and a crack at the mountain, we passed Gunnar.

"Gunnar, aren't you going to try some climbing?" we'd ask.

"Oh no," he'd say, dropping a sack of potatoes on the ground near his tent. "I must return to Chalten to pick up some more potatoes. I think if I go down again tonight, I can bring them all up by the end of the week."

Gunnar spent the bulk of his time wrangling his precious potatoes, counting them, then recounting them, scrubbing and peeling, boiling and baking. "The Fitz" was reportedly his climbing objective, but apparently there was nothing nearly as satisfying as having spent a day washing and primping 70 potatoes. If he grew bored with his potatoes, he'd start cooking other things. Gunnar could charm the socks off the local gauchos, and about once a week he'd wander back into Rio Blanco with a lamb he'd extracted from one of Chalten's cowboys. Then, he'd set about organizing a party. Gunnar loved parties. He organized a party for Christmas, for New Year's Eve, and several parties because he was bored. But his real coup de grâce was his 28th birthday party, a wild feast held in a farmyard outside Chalten, where he took reservations and a $6 contribution from any climber who wanted to attend. Needless to say, potatoes were the featured side dish. But Gunnar was happy—he'd found his purpose and he cherished his role as party host cum restaurateur cum chef.

Then there was Jim. Jim was in Patagonia with one of Europe's best-known climbers but felt he shouldn't be there, since he hadn't the skills or experience for serious mountaineering. He'd never even walked across a glacier. Jim was a nervous, insecure wreck.

Jim and his introspective misgivings allowed us all to play psychologist, and he gave us the platform from which we could offer tidbits of wisdom and positive thoughts. He was the patient, and we were the doctors, nursing his bruised mind back to normal health without, we hoped, losing our own stable mental ground.

If, God forbid, we ever woke up in the morning and wondered what the hell we were doing there, it was easy to focus on Jim. We'd get up, have our morning coffee and oatmeal, and casually sprint over to Jim's tent so we could begin offering observations and insights. If two of the camp's budding psychologists arrived at Jim's tent at the same time, it was usually not a problem. Most of us in the newly formed Rio Blanco Psychological Association (and Ward) seemed to be in agreement, and so double-teaming Jim was essentially the same thing as getting a second opinion.

"Dr. Charlie, what do you think?"

"I think Jim will do fine on that crevasse-riddled glacier, Dr. Cam."

"Just got to step over all the bodies, eh Dr. Charlie?"

"And outrun the avalanches, Dr. Cam."

"Say, Jim. Mind if we borrow some of your gear since you don't quite know how it works anyway? Those are some lovely new crampons."

And so it went.

I remember one time, in late December, when a disagreement did occur between two psychologists, but a third happened to be wandering back from washing his underwear and was able to break the tie fairly promptly. Like Gunnar, Jim, in his own way, had his niche. Others found their own roles to play.

My friend Julian, a dentist from Newcastle, became the local news service. He had both an irrepressible restlessness about him and a wonderful, funny ability to socialize in multiple languages, so he'd spend each day wandering around camp gathering the news and distributing it—often simultaneously. Back in the tent, Charlie and I would grill him into the wee hours on what the Italians were doing, or how high the French had fixed their ropes.

Harry and Kari (their real names!) were from Finland, and were trying to make the first Finnish ascent of Fitzroy. They were the Finnish version of the *Two Ronnies*[2]. Harry was a bricklayer, and told us all about cheating the Finnish government, from dodging taxes to getting unemployment benefits. Kari, meanwhile, worked for the government and explained how the government was continually developing new techniques for catching tax evaders and welfare cheats. Had their complementary strengths been in terms of climbing ability, they would have been mountain supermen. As it was, they seemed to spend a lot of time in their tent talking about Finnish government policies.

2. A phenomenally popular English comedy series that aired from 1966 to 1987, starring Ronnie Corbett and Ronnie Barker.

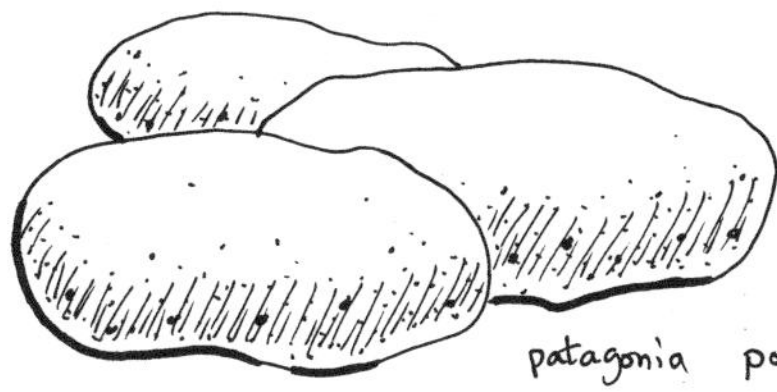

Jay, a professional climber from the States, had so much experience actually reaching the summits of these hard Patagonian peaks that he became, essentially, a consultant to every other Rio Blanco resident, a Yoda among pubescent Jedi warriors. His tent—a bright yellow North Face version of a circus tent, which we affectionately called "the big top"—only confirmed his massive status.

There were gourmet chefs and talented carpenters, gear repairmen and wine stewards, photographers and videographers, message carriers and dishwashers, and, of course, entertainers of all sorts. As the weeks dragged by, everyone slowly settled into a role, no matter how ill-defined the role. In short, we'd all escaped to Patagonia, but needed an escape from the escape. The roles were often muddled. Gunnar was the best cook for miles, but we each took a shot at making some tasty gem. Some of the more experimental culinary creations remained experiments.

I spent days mulling over my own skills and wondering how I could put them to community service. My contribution was a ratty collection of guidebooks, topos, maps, and the spiral notebook I'd bought for $8 in Rio Gallegos (this was back when the Argentine peso was pegged to the U.S. dollar). The topos, photocopied from the pages of Buscaini and Metzeltin's famous book *Patagonia*, held precious information that every Rio Blanco resident wanted to know. It didn't matter that the topos were a decade old, were printed with Italian climbing ratings, and that a zillion new routes had been established since they were drawn. All that mattered was that the topo looked vaguely like a mountain someone was thinking about climbing.

With each curious visitor to the tent, I'd hem and haw over their request, dig through reams of photocopies and finally pull out the desired route diagram and a clean sheet of white paper on which it could be drawn. I felt vastly satisfied every time a would-be ascensionist wandered away from the tent with a shred of white paper in hand, ready to take on Patagonia's finest. My pile of information became my domain, the one place within base camp I ruled supreme. I had nautical maps showing the Patagonian coastline, books about trekking around the mountains, informal sketches of the peaks copied from tourist maps, and photocopied pages from every *American Alpine Journal* published in the past ten years. It could take me days to find a topo that was in my pile. Occasionally, I would hike down to Chalten, where a popular pub had vast reams of notes on routes, peaks and ascents, to update my files.

Of course, in Patagonia, the weather destroys everyone's life and their escape from it. When it cleared up for a couple of days in mid-January, Gunnar couldn't sit around base camp peeling potatoes. He had to go climbing. Jim couldn't sit around feeling out of place on a glacier after a hundred eager psychologists had found him fit for mountaineering. He had to go climbing. We all did, and with varying degrees of success we managed to become Patagonian climbers for one great historical day.

After that, the skies turned on us, and moisture of all classification sputtered out of the heavens in a never-ending drizzle. Everything in camp received a slow, thorough soaking, and my precious library was reduced to a soggy heap of pulp. As each day dragged toward our imminent departure, I spent despondent afternoons picking out the most destroyed maps, carefully wadding them up, and tossing them into a firepit.

On the last day, I handed over the remaining pages and books to Kari, who promised he would take over the role of camp librarian. Of course, with all the text in English and Italian, and the ratings in French and Italian, and most of the pages utterly soaked, he was looking at either a hell of lot of sorting work, or rolling a record-breaking spitball.

At the end of January, we went home. Julian returned to England and his dentistry; Charlie went back to his computers and winter climbing in Scotland; Jay packed up and went back to his professional climbing adventures; Harry and Kari returned to Finland and their government; Gunnar went back to Germany, and his clock-making; and Jim went back to California and checked himself into a clinic. I returned to my newspaper's deadlines, headlines and high stress. But for a few precious weeks, I had been the best librarian in Patagonia. Able to pull information out of a disor-

ganized heap of paper at the drop of a hat. Able to steer a disoriented climber to the foot of his proposed goal. Able to shed a little light on the mysteries of the peaks around us.

Maybe mountaineering in Patagonia really isn't about climbing at all. Maybe it's about something more basic. Escaping from the escape. Finding a role, no matter how trivial. Pretending to be a contributing member of society even when you don't know what that means. If I had a little more time, I might try to solve the mysterious lure of Patagonia's famed peaks and the weird, social and anti-social side effects.

As for right now, I've got to start digging. An Italian friend wants a diagram of Fitzroy's Cassarotto Route.

Touching the 'Roid

(Peru, 2000)

"Four poor bearded tramps, greasy and hungry, who are trying to cheat the endless tropical night. To forget their cold, their weariness, their thirst, their discomfort; to forget, too, how slowly the minutes pass, and not even look at their watches ... it's funny to think that they are living the happiest moments of their climbing days."

—Georges Kogan, *The Ascent of Alpamayo*

Ponder this simple question a moment and see if you can come up with an answer: what is an *expedition*? Is it an event? That doesn't seem quite correct, as expeditions can encompass any number of events all strung together. Is it an action? There are many actions and subactions in an expedition: walking, sitting, traveling, eating, climbing and humping loads. Is it people? I've been on expeditions with people who have split off from our group and gone climbing with members of other expeditions, thereby negating the idea that a specific group is key. (Then again, I've been on expeditions with guys who have split off from humanity and joined the ranks of the sasquatch, thereby negating the term people.) I think expeditions are a little bit of everything. The word is a noun, to be sure, but it's a kind of fourth-dimensional noun, one that involves process, movement, characters and places. A bit like a travelling circus or a drifting ship, going somewhere, taking time to do it, and leaving behind another world.

Of course, in this day and age, the word *expedition* sounds a little heavy. With cut-rate plane fares to every airport on every continent, online video examination of every peak, pass and puja from here to Timbuktu, the word *expedition* seems far too formal. It sounds very serious—like something British Everesters were doing in the 1920s. *Trip* is a much better word. It's lighthearted. It sums up your attitude when you're on an overseas climbing excursion. *Expedition* sounds like you're planning to sit around in wooden camp chairs swatting flies on an elephant's bum and drinking tea from a silver tea service while the underpaid locals you've hired cook up seven-course meals. *Trip*, on the other hand, sounds like you've fallen down and are trying to get back up again. I'd rather go on a *trip*.

There is nothing quite like a big climbing trip, especially a big international climbing trip. And, predictably, the best big overseas climbing trips always turn out to be the ones to places you've never been, where you can't speak the language, where the mountains are wild-looking and have exotic names, and where the political situation is in disarray. Pop open your typical atlas, and many such places come galloping to mind—Kashmir, Afghanistan, the Faroffistans of the former Soviet Union, and most South American nations. The choices are many and varied.

In early 2000, Peru was going through the political equivalent of dry-heaving. In May, under then-President Alberto Fujimori, the nation held some supposedly democratic elections but many Peruvians questioned the authenticity of the vote count. They had good reason given the president's history. Fujimori had come to power in 1992, and with the support of the military he had dissolved the Peruvian congress and courts and seized dictatorial powers. He quashed various left-wing rebel factions, which were blamed for thousands of deaths and bringing the country to the brink of chaos.

"To his supporters, Mr. Fujimori is the man who saved Peru from the twin evils of terrorism and economic collapse," reported the British Broadcasting Corporation (BBC) in November 2000. "To his opponents, he is an authoritarian strongman who has ridden roughshod over the country's democratic institutions in order to preserve his hold on power." Whether you liked or hated Fujimori, his own tough form of democracy appeared about to be replaced with something else—probably, in typical South American style, via a revolution or a coup.

Thus it was that my dear friend Jordan Campbell thought a quick climbing trip to Peru made a lot of sense: we hadn't been; our little group of friends could barely speak Spanish; there were wild mountains and nutty politics. And, Peru was a hell of a lot cheaper than Kashmir, Afghanistan and the Faroffistans of the former Soviet Union.

Jordan's plan was simple: nip down and back in three weeks, bag a few 20,000-foot peaks (Alpamayo, Quiteraju, and Artesonraju, for example) and be home in time for summer rock climbing in the high country. This seemed quite an ambitious goal. All the big mountain trips I'd been on up to that point had required at least a week's worth of travel just to get to the mountain, then another week's worth of acclimatization at the very least.

I didn't really know that much about Peru before our trip, but Alpamayo sure sounded lovely—like a creamy topping for dog food, or a high altitude ruin. I pulled open an atlas and delved further. I was immediately struck by the names of the mountain ranges in Peru.

There's a range called the Cordillera Vilcabamba and another called the Cordillera Huayhuash (pronounced "why wash?"); there are ranges named Tunshu and Raura; Huallanca ("wallanka") and Huagaruncho ("wagarunko"). These names were so instantly appealing and lyrical, it seemed to me Peru's mountain cartographers must be moonlighting as salsa musicians.

Likewise, the individual mountains are a magical harmony of rajus and alcas: Taulliraju, Artesonraju, Chacraraju, Quiteraju, Pucaraju, Uruashraju, Tumarinaraju, Tullparaju, Juchuraju, Huamashraju, Palcaraju, Mururaju, Tocllaraju, Vallunaraju, Paqcharaju, Ranrapalca, Ocshapalca, Cajavilca, Pucaganga, and Cancaraca. There's Tuco, Pisco, Santon, Cashan, Choco, Copap, Churup, Copa, Vicos, Cayesh, Pastoruri, Contrahierbas, Huandoy, Chopicalqui, and Carhuallun. Who could possibly turn these lyrical names down? That'd be a sin—like comparing Julie Andrews to Snoop Doggy Dog.

"Perhaps the most famous mountain in Peru is Alpamayo," wrote British mountaineer John Cleare is his popular book *World Guide to Mountains and Mountaineering*. "From the northwest it appears a steep pyramid of ice. From the southwest, it is an immaculate trapezoid of tapering ice flutings and has been likened to a white cathedral." Hmm ... ice flutings? Is that safe? Wasn't it somewhere round there that Joe Simpson had his little *Touching the Void*[3] ordeal? Is this advisable?

Alpamayo has an interesting history. In 1948, a Swiss expedition attempted to make the first ascent of the peak—they failed. In 1950, a few years after the Swiss attempt, a book called *Cordillera Blanca—Peru,* by two climbers named Kinzl and Schneider, was published showing the still-unclimbed Alpamayo. After the book came out, a Swiss mountaineering magazine held a contest to see which mountain on earth was "the most beautiful." The resounding response—Alpamayo, even though it had only been properly photographed a few years previously. That an unclimbed mountain in the Cordillera Blanca—which looks very similar to all the other mountains in the Cordillera Blanca—beat out such peaks as Switzerland's own Eiger and Matterhorn is quite remarkable.

The first ascent of Alpamayo came in 1951, when the creatively-titled "Franco-Belgian Expedition to the Andes" traveled to South America for a summer's climbing. The group consisted of Georges Kogan and his wife, Claude; Maurice Lenoir; Jean Guillemin; Jacques Jongen; Raymond

3. Joe Simpson's first book, describing a climbing trip to Peru in which, after summitting a steep 21,000-foot mountain, he falls into a crevasse and breaks his leg. His partner, Simon Yates, leaves him. During the next three days, while Yates is overcome with guilt and grief in base camp, Simpson manages to crawl down the mountain and save himself.

Leininger and his wife, Nicole; and André and René Mallieux.

While four of the men (Lenoir, Jongen, Georges Kogan and Raymond Leininger) made the first ascent of Alpamayo, the two women, Claude Kogan and Nicole Leininger, spent several days exploring possible routes to the top of Quiteraju. A day after the four fellows returned from reaching the top of Alpamayo, the group turned its attention to Quiteraju. Several "three-man" rope teams climbed the peak, including the rope team of Claude Kogan and Nicole Leininger. The two women reached the summit around three p.m. "It is the first time a purely female party has climbed a peak of 20,000 feet," Leininger later wrote. Quiteraju later became known as Lady's Peak.

A few weeks before our departure, Jordan convened a small meeting of our group's members (Jordan, Rick Leonidas, Ace Kvale and myself) in Telluride, ostensibly to discuss our trip to Peru and to get to know each other better with a one-day ski traverse from Ophir to Telluride. Discussing the trip to Peru was pretty easy after Jordan produced several six-packs of beer. In fact, the only real discussion centered on a name for what we were doing, and somehow the word *expedition* crept back into things. Ace came up with the fanciful "Touching the 'Roid Expedition" in honor of Simpson's book *Touching the Void*, yet with relevant overtones to the extreme gastrointestinal distress that accompanies every journey to Latin America. We all liked that name, but Jordan felt we needed a proper, more publishable name, free of quasi-scatalogical references, so he hit on the "Condor Expedition to Peru." The word *expedition*—it is easily argued—makes a trip sound official. With that difficult business completed, we focused on the beer and an enjoyable videotape of Jordan's last big climbing trip—to Thalay Sagar in the Garwhal region of the Indian Himalaya with a group of British climbers. Ironically, the best portions of it were filmed in Scotland because the BBC wanted close-ups.

The Ophir-to-Telluride ski traverse the following day turned out to be less than perfect, and I wondered if it was a harbinger of things the "Touching the 'Roid/Condor Expedition to Peru" might suffer once lost in South America. After we'd all climbed a high ridge above Ophir, I learned I had grabbed my wife's skis by accident, and that they could not be adjusted to fit my boots. I was forced to return to Ace's Ophir cabin while the rest of the guys skied happily off toward Telluride. Still, I had just created the surely-destined-to-be-popular Ophir-to-Ophir Ski Traverse—which can even be done without skis. Certainly, without brains.

A month later Jordan, Rick and I assembled at the airport in Denver. Ace had had to drop out (some minor magazine called *National Geographic* had called with an assignment) so we had enlisted Charlie French, an English climber Jordan and I both knew well. We loaded up the United Airlines jet with several hundred duffel bags of unnecessary stuff, and flew south, into the night. The Touching the 'Roid/Condor Expedition was officially underway. (Drum roll, please.)

If you've ever been to Latin America by plane, you know one ironclad rule: arrival is always at night. Our plane coasted to the terminal, and we stood in a line of tired, frustrated, anxious, pissed-off and half-drunk people before disembarking into the blackness. (Remember, this was before September 11—in that age when airline passengers were perpetually belligerent.) We wrangled our herd of duffel bags through customs and before long we were standing on a dark pavement below some five-foot-tall blue words that said "something-something-something-aeropuerto."

When you arrive on a late flight in a Latin American city, the taxi drivers know you're tired, frustrated, anxious, pissed-off and half-drunk. So, in what appears to be an idiotic effort to make you feel welcome in their city, they grab your luggage and start dragging it off in different directions, across toothy concrete, filthy gutters and fetid street debris. I don't know if the Lima Tourist Board promotes this sort of activity, but as I watched our thin, soft nylon luggage dragged away in six different directions across several types of hard gritty surfaces, I imagined myself in an interview with one of these raucous taximen:

"So, dragging tourists' luggage across rough ground is good for business?"

"Si, Señor!"

"Even though this tourist has no desire to ride with you and even less so now that you've ripped his luggage to shreds?"

"Si, Señor! No problemo!"

"Why do you drive a taxi, anyway?"

"No work in rocket science today, Señor!"

Hmm … of course. If the Lima Tourist Board expanded the local rocket science factory, hundreds of tourists might be spared shredded luggage. I decided then and there that I'd write a letter to someone about it.

Of course, with Fujimori's political heaving set to crack Peru apart, Lima was a little scary. Painted red and white with political slogans and party endorsements, it seemed ready for something revolutionary, something crazy. We spent a night at a small hotel by the airport, and in the morning jumped on a bus bound for the mountains. As we rolled out of Lima, we shut our minds and stared into our books, least we be associated with any rabble of U.S.-supported rebels.

Mountain climbing expeditions (trips) are all about camaraderie. You pick the personality combinations you like, you decline the potential time bombs. If you're lucky, as I was, you're just swapping partners. Jordan had been with Charlie on Thalay Sagar, a wild peak in the Himalaya. I'd been with Charlie in Patagonia. Rick had climbed fourteeners in Colorado with me. Jordan had rock-climbed with Rick in Boulder. We knew each other's girlfriends and wives. We knew each other's underwear colors and farting styles. It was—as it always is—a mix of people drawn together by a common, if distant and unseen, goal.

After you've put your desired group together, climbing trips are still a four-dimensional experience, somewhat like ships at sea. They float around, like the Minnow in *Gilligan's Island*, occasionally bumping into other ships that are also lost, bobbing here and there on an ocean of humanity, transportation and tilted geography, before hopefully finding a solid mooring on the side of a mountain. At least, that's one lyrical way to look at it. Our bus rolled north and east, through the Cordillera Negra, a small range that parallels the Cordillera Blanca. At the village of Conococha, we entered the high, wide Rio Santa Valley on the east side of the Cordillera Blanca. Suddenly, there were many big, white, scary-looking mountains staring down at us.

If you've never been to Huaraz, go now! Jump down offa that seat and roll before it's all messed up by the popularity of trekking and mountain climbing and people like us, who are just like you and think we're so darned unique because we climb mountains. Huaraz is a small, rough-edged city of 80,000, sitting at 10,000 feet in a valley between the Cordillera Blanca and the Cordillera Negra. Huaraz looks like an adolescent who's been beaten up—in a way, it is.

In 1941, an avalanche fell into a lake in the Negra sending millions of tons of debris flowing down onto Huaraz. Five thousand people were killed and the center of town was flattened. In 1970, a massive earthquake shook much of Central Peru, wiping out an estimated 30,000 Huaraz residents and destroying 90 percent of the city. When you walk around Huaraz, two things come to mind: one, this is a climbing town (there are more equipment shops than in Boulder and Denver combined), and two, the buildings look like they could collapse in a light breeze. This place is rough.

We *did* Huaraz. We bought those pointy Peruvian wool hats that were such a Boulder/Aspen/Park City/Taos/Jackson/Sonora/Santa Fe/Vail/Mammoth/Sun Valley/Missoula/Breckenridge status symbol in the early

1980s. We drank beer in the pubs. We shopped for vegetables and rice, and bartered with burro drivers (*arreiros*). We took photos of ourselves doing expedition things, and pretty soon … we had wasted craploads of film.

The next day, we drove up to the village of Cashapampa, and headed into the Blanca.

The Cordillera Blanca is gorgeous and dramatic—consider these dimensions: the range is barely 15 miles wide (in many places it's less than ten miles wide), it rises from valleys on either side that are anywhere between 6,000 and 10,000 feet in elevation, and its tallest peaks are over 22,000 feet. The Blanca is, for all intents and purposes, one big fin made up of smaller, fin-shaped peaks. When you wander into the Blanca, your neck is constantly craned back to a point where your chin becomes the apex of your head.

"Is that our mountain?"

"Nope."

"That?"

"Is that it?"

"Nope."

"Man, my neck hurts."

"Mine too."

And so you end up watching your feet as they patter into basecamp. That's what I loved most about this trip: I got to see my feet in this wild and exotic mountain range. Maybe I'd get to see some mountains, too—my neck would just have to suffer.

Base camp was quite civilized. It was nestled in the crook of a high valley at 14,000 feet, just below the point where treeline becomes rockline. There was grass and flat spots for tents, and we quickly set up our own little nylon village. Base camps are the best part of climbing trips, but also the strangest. Think about it: dozens of people living in temporary shelters no thicker than a pair of Speedoes, located in areas of the globe with potentially deadly environments. Now, I'm not one to complain, but didn't our ancestors—Cro-Magnon man, for example—bust their butts to evolve from this sort of existence thousands of years ago? And if you really think about it, wasn't Cro-Magnon man smart enough to live in a cave? Dwelling under flimsy nylon seems a rather large step backward.

Speaking of Cro-Magnon man—in recent times he's been given a pretty good boost by anthropologists. "They were skilled hunters, toolmakers and artists," wrote one anthropologist. "Their upper Paleolithic culture produced a markedly more sophisticated tool kit, using a wider variety of raw materials such as bone and antler, and containing new implements for making clothing, engraving, and sculpting. They produced fine artwork, in the form of decorated tools, beads, ivory carvings of humans and animals, shell jewelry, clay figurines, musical instruments, and polychrome cave paintings of exceptional vitality."

Gazing around base camp, I saw bedraggled men in underwear laboring over steel pots with handfuls of streambed gravel. Periodically, each looked upward at the sky with a strained, uncomfortable squint that indicated pure bewilderment. While I was wistfully reflecting on basecamps and the history of human development, a loud "whap" sound echoed through the air above our heads—the sort of sound a large sheet of fabric makes when it has been caught by the wind and flopped in a new direction. Apparently, a camp stove had exploded, taking with it the dark, furry brow of a climber from Argentina. Clearly, our generation hadn't mastered fire.

Base camps are also the places where you check out who's going up the mountain. Most folks in base camps, you quickly learn, rarely set foot on any mountain. Ninety-five percent of them are trekkers, not climbers. Of the other five percent (climbers), half are so bewildered by their new environment they seize up with the sudden realization they have very little experience and absolutely no clue as to what the individual steps for reaching a mountaintop are. A German team camped near us. They were running low on food and were on the verge of self-destruction. We needed water-purification drops, so we traded for a big salami.

"Das ees gud ya!" one of the Germans said while waving the huge cylinder of meat around in the air after I'd handed it to him. "Ya!"

Okay, buddy. Just put the salami down and no one gets hurt …

Some young Irish lads arrived late on our second night, full of big talk. They were trying to do Alpamayo in three days from the trailhead. They carried no tents or sleeping bags, and lay down on the wet grass to sleep, their Gore-Tex shells, fleeces, and duvets their only protection from the cold. It began raining around midnight, so they crawled into the official Parque Huascaran toilets—poop-spattered concrete stalls with holes in the floor.

There was a big commercial guided group led by Willie Benegas, a powerful Argentinean guide who'd climbed Alpamayo ten times. Then there was a small group of Chileans, strapping lads with loads of energy. There were teams of climbers from all over the world, many of whom seemed to know very little about climbing, or, in fact, that they were in Peru.

We spent a couple of nights lounging around basecamp, playing Go Fish with a deck of pornographic playing cards, sampling the local food, and enjoying life-altering bouts of diarrhea (that explains those concrete stalls), but most of all sucking in lungfuls of that clean, thin air. Then we began the serious business of carrying gear up the mountain and acclimatizing.

At 16,000 feet, Camp One was just above the point where the treeline meets the rockline, on a moraine. It wasn't as comfy as the grass, but at least we were getting some exercise in the breathing department. The Chilean lads camped nearby, as did the Germans with our old friend the salami. Just as we were getting ready to go higher, it stormed. In fact, it stormed day and night for the better part of a week—apparently rare for Peru. As we ate most of our mountain food, other groups ran out of food entirely. The Chileans turned back. The German team imploded after one of the group's members made a solo attempt and apparently ended up eating the entire salami.

Low on food, we decided (of course) to go up higher. We spent a highly entertaining night climbing steep snow and ice by headlamp and looking for Camp Two among some very deep and very dark crevasses. We reached a flat area we thought might be Camp Two about two a.m.

Camp Two, at 18,000 feet, is where you put on your running shoes, so to speak. From this point, it was just a 2,000-foot sprint to the top of the mountain. We spent one night at Camp Two, our heads swimming and our bowels cranking. The next morning, we crunched out of camp and stomped through fresh snow, wondering whether it would be the blue or the white patches of sky that would dominate our day. Struggling up steep, snowy slopes at 18,000 feet, our chests heaved and our heads throbbed. Then it was onto the route.

Our chosen line of ascent was called the Ferrari Route, named after Casimiro Ferrari, a bold Italian climber of the 1970s. The Ferrari Route sounds sporty, like a wild time in Monaco, but it's not. It's a lot more on the moderate side of things than it sounds—a bit more Volkswagen Beetle than flashy red sportscar. We reached the top and sat around the summit tied to a complex maze of alpine climbing gear that reminded me more of tangled fishing tackle than anything else. We rappelled off Alpamayo in the ever-present clouds. There was no argument, little frustration. We were in awe of the beauty of the mountains.

We got back to Camp Two and plopped into some chairs we'd carved in the snow. As we cooked up crunchy pasta and cold sauce, many new arrivals came stomping into Camp Two. A group of three climbers crested the nearby col, between Camps One and Two, and descended to the flat area where our tents were pitched. They said hello, then erected two tents. Behind them were four more climbers who did the same thing. Then came a group of three, followed by another group of four. Before the sun set, we were in the midst of a veritable tent city.

The crowd at Camp Two wasn't that bad. Its effects on the local environment, however, were. As night descended, it became apparent that the meager restroom facilities that had served us thus far (i.e., a small pit in the snow) would have to be enlarged for the masses. Before we could even fathom the drudgery that would involve, some eager fellow with heaps of energy had already done it—a series of pits and holes the length of a Roman Bath. The title of our expedition was looking uncannily appropriate.

There was a terrible omission, however, in the new facilities—the builder had supplied no walls. Every time a climber went over to use it, the rest of us in Tent City were treated to a series of blow-by-blow facial expressions. Some people looked like they were being strangled. One thing that's always bothered me about mountaineering is how well you get to know your fellow climbers' restroom habits and facial expressions.

In the morning, Camp Two had morphed from Tent City into Tent Megalopolis. We watched about 30 climbers cram onto the Ferrari Route and knock bits of ice and other debris down on each others' heads. While we ate oatmeal and packed up to leave, more people arrived for a try at the mountain. Camp Two bulged. Those already there and waiting saw they would have less of a chance as more and more people arrived. In the commercial guided groups, many guides declined to go for the summit, making their clients very angry. Tempers flared and the f word made multiple appearances. It was like the stuff I'd read about Everest, yet here it was on a very modest but beautiful mountain—that still sounded like a creamy topping for dog food—in the middle of the Cordillera Blanca. Peaks just next door had no one on them. We knew Alpamayo was popular, but we had little idea that along with Aconcagua, Huascaran and a couple of other peaks, that Alpamayo is probably one of the top five most popular mountains in South America among climbers.

Unfortunately, the lengthy storm precluded us from climbing another mountain. Like so many, our time had been gobbled up with sitting in tents playing pornographic Go Fish and waiting for the weather to clear. We didn't have enough time or food to make up for the deficit. We descended to base camp, and hoofed it out to Huaraz.

Back in Huaraz, I began photographing the locals. The traditional Peruvian woman with their colorful skirts and big top hats, sitting on the sides of the narrow streets selling oranges and potatoes, were a fascinating subject. It turned out they don't like having their pictures taken. "Most people resent having a camera thrust in their faces and people in markets will often proudly turn their backs on pushy photographers," wrote Rob Rachowiecki in his travel guide to Peru. (Yeah, no kidding, Robbo. But I wasn't pushy, and I certainly wasn't thrusting.) In fact, they liked it so little that they began throwing potatoes and oranges at me. This was pretty unique—not too many cultures have a tradition where you toss fruits and vegetables at tourists—but then again, this was better than the game of Newly-Arrived-Tourist-Luggage-Thrashing going on down at the Lima airport. I had to wonder what the Peru Tourist Council was teaching the good people.

Anyway, being a sports fan, I threw the potatoes back. I tossed them gently, so the women could catch them. Then I hung around waiting for a full-blown game of something to develop, but it didn't. The top-hatted women simply ignored me. I wandered off to look for other sports involving airborne tubers and fruits.

If you've had a good trip, going home can be hard. Especially if you've had fun with your friends, didn't kill each other, didn't die, and especially if you've climbed something. It means putting an end to this trip, this noun, this experience, this thing. Whatever it was, and however you felt about it doesn't matter anymore. It is winding down and ceasing to exist. Nothing can revive it. Gone, dead, kaput! For us it was, so to speak, the end of the 'Roid.

Everyone gives different reasons for going on climbing trips. A lot of people give some pretty high-minded philosophical reasons—inner peace and reflection, challenge and excitement, experience and camaraderie. I've heard big wall climbers explain that they go climbing because they were getting too comfy on the couch. They beat themselves up on a wall, then come home to the couch for a spell. They get too lazy, so they go out again—a vicious cycle thing. I've heard non-outdoorsy folks discuss how they go on trekking trips to see if they can meet certain specified challenges, to see if they can put up with ten nights in a tent and camp food, to see if they have the mettle to complete a challenge. Climbing trips have made me realize something much more simple. They've made me realize that there's a whole wide world out there of interesting people and cultures, mountains and geographic regions, fruits and vegetables, and international headgames involving salamis and potatoes.

In the end, everyone will have their own reasons for journeying halfway around the globe and spending thousands of dollars to sleep in nylon domes and eat crunchy pasta. I go now because I simply want to see it. No pictures in any book ever do the mountains justice. They don't do the sunsets or the smog justice either, and never has a photo properly caught the spirit of a moment. After skimming through a pile of books on South America, Peru's mountains looked so darn cool I figured they'd be fantastic in real life. Any hassle to get there would be worth it. Even if I was just walking past, or riding a bus up the Rio Santa Valley, that would've been okay. The main thing was, I wanted to go and have a look. And to me, that's what a trip is all about.

ACROSS GREAT OCEANS

The Sydney-to-Hobart Yacht Race Backwards or In the Footsteps of the Liberty Men

(Australia, 1987)

"The mate was a mighty sailor man, the skipper brave and sure."
—From the Theme to *Gilligan's Island*

The quaint city of Hobart, Australia's second oldest city, sits astride the Derwent River on the southeastern corner of Tasmania. It's best known as one of Australia's foremost penal settlements, and during the late 18th and early 19th centuries it was a bustling hub of the British Commonwealth, one of the key centers of the empire's corrections system. Hobart is also the end-point for Australia's best-known offshore yachting event, the annual Sydney-to-Hobart yacht race. I never realized the two historical facts were related until I became a sailor.

In early 1988, I was wrapping up a month-long backpacking tour of southeastern Australia by exploring Tasmania. Fortunately for me, the bulk of my aunts, uncles and cousins still live on the island where my parents grew up, and I had no problem catching rides from town to town while traversing the island. In Hobart, however, my life took a decided turn for the different.

My sister, a Sydney doctor, has a collection of doctor friends who are heavily involved in offshore yacht racing. A group of these doctors had just flown home after the Sydney-to-Hobart race, and Skipper Geoff Cramp needed a crew to get the boat home. Somehow, thanks to Sis, my name had come up in a few Sydney hospital conversations.

In Hobart's Constitution Dock, I wandered among some of the most expensive racing yachts conceived. A gigantic vessel named *Sovereign*, latest winner of Australia's most famous race, was the centerpiece of the entire dock. Tourists mulled about, taking in its gleaming red hull, its perfectly folded sails, and its sparkling clean mechanical systems.

I strolled past looking for Skipper Cramp and came upon a tiny, weather-beaten fiberglass dinghy with ratty sails, or so it seemed after *Sovereign*. Geoff Cramp, a big guy with an easy smile, sat upon this boat, *Sweet Lauraine*, fiddling with a green rope. Every time he moved more than a few inches, the entire boat rolled with him. I introduced myself, and we got down to business.

I explained that since I had bought a one-way plane ticket to Tasmania, I needed to find a way off the island. I had about $20 Australian left in my wallet and my Commonwealth Bank balance was in the low double digits. Whatever I had planned for my retreat back to Sydney had to center around cheap transportation. Free was even better. I assured Geoff I was solid, seaworthy material, and rattled off a list of previous sailing exploits: the Faucet-to-Towel-Rack Run in the bathtub at age three; a traverse of the local duck pond with my toy sailboat at age eight, across the deep end of the Tollasepps's Pool on an inflatable mattress at ten.

Geoff squinted at me: "Do you know where the bow is?"

"Up front, right?"

"Good enough for this trip. Do you get seasick?"

"Never!"

"Welcome aboard then."

Somehow, this accountant-turned-yacht-racing veteran had decided I was deserving of pity, and he yanked my backpack up onto deck. "Get this below, then I've got some grocery shopping for you," he said.

After purchasing $300 worth of food and loading it in the tiny galley, I climbed onto the deck where I met a collection of other, non-race-material sailors, guys like myself who could be trusted only to get a boat back from a big race, not to work in the race itself. I untied several lines, and Geoff cranked the small motor that would carry us out into Hobart's Storm Bay. There, the sails were raised, and we picked up speed as we chugged toward the mighty South Pacific.

I climbed up on the bow's steel railing and began singing the theme song to *Gilligan's Island*, swinging my hooked arm jig-style and feeling proud that I was about to become part of Tasmanian sailing history. And, Tasmania does have a truly great sailing legacy. Heck, being an island, its entire history revolves around things nautical.

On November 24, 1642, Dutch sailor and explorer Abel Tasman sighted a previously unknown coastline on Australia's southern extremity. Tasman named the area he saw Van Diemen's Land, after Anthony Van Diemen, governor general of the East Indies. At the time, Tasman had no idea Van Diemen's Land was an island, nor that a couple of centuries later, in 1855, the island would have its name changed to honor him.

In 1798, two British sailors, George Bass and Matthew Flinders, circumnavigated Van Diemen's Land, ascertaining that it was indeed an island and not merely a peninsula jutting south from the Victorian mainland, something that had been suspected by many early explorers. Other famed explorer-sailors came and went, each leaving his indelible mark in the history books, and most were rewarded with having bays, peninsulas and islands named in their honor. Tasman even had the sea between Australia and New Zealand named in his honor.

But ironically, what I consider Tasmania's greatest piece of sailing history has nothing to do with exploration, and the men who pulled it off are completely unknown to most Australians. In early 1834, ten convicts in a soon-to-be-closed prison on Tasmania's West Coast overpowered their British guards and pirated a ship called the *Frederick.* The convicts managed to gain control of the *Frederick* without any of themselves or the guards being injured or killed (of which they were extremely proud) and then divided up the remaining food rations, leaving a proportionate share with the British military guards who were left sitting contentedly on a beach.

The convicts, who later earned the nickname the Liberty Men, then spent six grueling weeks traversing the South Pacific before landing near Valdivia, Chile, some 500 miles south of Santiago.

It is quite remarkable that the ten Liberty Men survived. They had no nautical instruments, very little food, and for the entire six-week journey, the *Frederick* was slowly sinking, taking on water so that a mechanical pump had to be manned full-time by two of the men. The sole sailor among the group, John Barker, remained below deck for much of the voyage suffering from interminable seasickness, and secretly estimating that the *Frederick* was thoroughly lost and that everyone would die. All of the men regarded their time on the *Frederick* as more dire than any period spent in prison.

After landing in Chile, the Liberty Men lived there for several years. They integrated into one of the Pacific coast towns and became important pillars of the community. They married and raised families. Then one day, years later, the Chilean government—in a political mood swing—decided to hand them over to the British government. They were shipped to London, loaded onto another convict transport, then taken back to Tasmania where they were tried for piracy, among other things. They were found guilty, imprisoned for a year in Tasmania, and, finally, in 1839, they were incarcerated for the rest of their lives on Norfolk Island, the dregs of Australia's early prison system. Their Chilean wives and children never saw them again.

As our boat *Sweet Lauraine* left Storm Bay and began rolling over huge open-sea swells, my rendition of the *Gilligan's Island* theme song was soon replaced by desperate retching over all four sides of the boat, much to the enjoyment of my shipmates. I began to understand what the non-sailing Liberty Men had felt when they likened their time onboard to hell on earth. I wanted off, and I wanted off bad, but I was to remain a prisoner for the next seven days and nights.

"Feeding the fish, eh Cam?" Geoff asked repeatedly throughout the first afternoon. "I'm surprised someone with your sailing experience isn't used to the rolling."

That night passed as a blur. With five "sailors" on board, Geoff had divided up the night's sailing into two-hour watches. Two of us would man the tiller and the sails for 120 minutes, until we were replaced by the next party. In the meantime, those not on deck were supposed to go below and sleep in any of the eight cramped and thoroughly soaked bunks. I was so ill that after an unsuccessful attempt at sleep—marred by retching down the front of a borrowed rubber sailing suit—I lolled around on deck all night like a half-drowned rabbit, utterly useless in the greater team plan.

Twenty-four hours after leaving Hobart, we cruised into Wine Glass Bay, an hourglass-shaped cove on the Freycinet Peninsula, a dramatically beautiful stretch of terra firma on Tasmania's East Coast. We sailed up into the center of the bay and dropped anchor near a ketch from London.

My shipmates dined on salads and soft drinks, while I sat groggily watching a few dolphins ply the water beneath us. Secretly I toyed with the idea of jumping ship, as, at that particular moment in history, one of my uncles happened to live in a tiny seaside village just a few miles north of Wine Glass Bay. I decided against the idea figuring that sooner or later I would get used to the constant motion.

After lunch, it was back into the waves and—no surprise here—I wasn't used to the motion at all. But it was too late to mutiny. *Sweet Lauraine* was committed to the marathon 280-mile jaunt across Bass Strait, the stretch of ocean lying between mainland Australia and Tasmania. Once the fish had received several large multi-course meals, I began to feel better. Slowly, as we tracked north and west past Flinders Island, I began to feel human again, and even ate a piece of fruit.

I soon found out why I was feeling better: The ocean had gone flat. Two nights and one day after leaving Wine Glass Bay, we were drifting aimlessly across a glassy surface showing barely a ripple. The five "novice" sailors onboard (I prefer the term *green*, in this case) wondered what to do, if anything. Skipper Geoff knew what to do—start up the onboard cruise activities. They included a knot-tying class, a sunburn competition, and a small-bits-of-cardboard-distance-throwing competition. The sole Briton on the boat, a pasty white fellow named Phil Beales, won the sunburn competition hands down, and spent the rest of the trip in a sort of arched sitting position, making certain that no object on the boat came in contact with his upper body. At least in our truly weird version of the Sydney-to-Hobart race, we were in first place.

Late on the fourth day, we sighted land. It was the Victorian coast, near Cape Howe, the mainland's most southeasterly point. We drifted slowly up the coast for a while, to a small fishing village named Eden, and sailed into port. I had completely overcome the seasickness, and by the time we pulled into Eden's dock, I felt 100 percent. As soon as I set foot on the dock, however, the entire world began rolling and heaving. I threw up several times on the walk into town—once again, I was a prisoner.

To the casual observer, Eden is backwoodsy Australia. It's a quaint little town with a dock, a main street and ... did I mention the dock already? But Eden's history is far deeper than the repeat episodes of *Neighbors* shining bright on local residents' television screens.

In 1818, the first whaling station in Australia was established at Eden, and it remained the premier whaling port until well into the 1930s. In the 1840s, a British entrepreneur named Benjamin Boyd came to Eden, and, on the shores of Twofold Bay, a large inlet just south of town, he began building a city (Boydtown) that he hoped would one day rival Sydney and be designated Australia's capital. Boydtown fell into disrepair, and is now little more than a collection of ruinous shacks and an historic hiccup. Most Australian tourists who visit Boydtown scoff at the idea of the Australian capital being built in such a remote location, but to Boyd's credit, he must have had an inkling of the political tension over a capital city that was to come. By 1901, Australian leaders were embroiled in a bitter debate over whether to build Australia's capital in Sydney or Melbourne. Members of parliament finally passed a law stating that Australia's capital had to be in New South Wales, but could be no closer than 100 miles to Sydney. Ironically, the new capital of Canberra was located not far from Boydtown.

In more modern times, the area around Eden has become a battleground for the conservation movement. Some of Australia's finest forests are found in this portion of the country and for decades they have been harvested to supply Asia's insatiable paper industry.

As the five of us from *Sweet Lauraine* wandered up Eden's main street, we noticed that a series of lectures was being offered about the local woodchip industry by some or other pro-timber organization. The situation was vaguely reminiscent of Montana, Idaho and Oregon, where local residents sometimes place placards in their front windows showing support for the timber industry.

We skipped all the highbrow culture and headed straight to the Fisherman's Club, a huge bar/restaurant/casino/nightclub with a circus-like atmosphere. The circus-like atmosphere, it seemed, was a result of the Fisherman's Club's screening of a documentary film called *Seafari* about—what else?—the ocean. Hundreds of Edenites were there for the event.

The crew of the *Sweet Lauraine* slept onboard that night, in the completely calm waters of Eden's harbor. By breakfast, my body had readjusted to zero motion and I was feeling well again, finally. Then, we set sail, and launched out into the Tasman Sea. I was sick as hell.

The Sydney-to-Hobart Yacht Race is a 630-mile event, even when it's done in reverse. By my rough calculations, we were well past halfway, but the second half was going to be the harder half. As soon as we hit the open sea, a storm rolled in from the south.

Ocean storms are perhaps the most frightening things one might ever encounter in life, and to this day, after dozens of conversations with sailors about electrical storms, I still have no idea how safe you are in a boat during one. As we tracked along the New South Wales coast, we watched the storm roll in from the south. The glassy water around Sweet Lauraine lasted to a point about a half mile away—beyond that, the sea was a boiling mass of waves. Lightening crackled down and hit the water a few hundred yards south of our position. The boiling mass drew nearer every minute, and I dreaded what might happen.

Mario, an anesthetist on our crew who fancied himself as a real sailor and not a member of the Gilligan Contingent, decided we ought to prepare for a possible lightning strike. He built a shroud out of two long pieces of cable, and attached these to the top of the mast. Skipper Cramp just rolled his eyes at me and laughed, "Damn doctors!"

When the gale finally caught our sails, we took off, accelerating from roughly two knots to (at times) 23 knots within a matter of seconds. Mario's shroud got tangled in some of the rigging, and after doing several frenzied, storm-driven nautical donuts, Geoff cut the shroud down and put *Lauraine* back on course. "Damn doctors!" he muttered again.

The storm was so fierce and the swells were so big that waves began crashing all the way across the deck, threatening to take several of us with them. We donned our harnesses, and clipped into various anchor points on the deck. Geoff ordered Phil and me to begin bailing, since several waves had found their way through the open hatch leading to the cabin. We lost sight of land, and as a huge wave deposited several hundred gallons of salt water down the front of my borrowed rubber suit (fortunately cleaning out a load of vomit in the process), a catchy jingle came to mind:

"The Minnow would be lost,
The Minnow would be lost."

Our ship didn't wash up on the shore of any deserted isle. We simply plowed on through the night, bailing, flailing and vomiting. In the wee hours of the following day, things had calmed enough that three members of the crew could go and sleep. Although my bunk was soaked—I was literally sleeping in a puddle—I drifted off into one of the soundest sleeps I've ever had, contentedly dreaming of Ginger and Marianne.

Two days later, and several hundred miles farther north, we cruised triumphantly into Port Jackson. Most yachts in the Sydney-to-Hobart Race take two to four days, the fastest time being held by *Nokia*, which set a record of one day, 19 hours, 48 minutes and 2 seconds in the 1999 race. (The 1999 race was distinctive for its exceptionally strong winds.) We'd taken seven long days and seven long nights. But we didn't mind. We were a team of non-sailors (someone called us the anti-sailors), and we'd done it without incident, accident or argument. Besides, if you considered a standard map of the world, we were going uphill all the way. The racers get to go down the coast.

Sweet Lauraine's owner had a little reception party going when we arrived, but as I climbed off the deck onto the dock, the ground began swaying dramatically. An elderly woman handed me a glass of champagne, but I handed it right back, said good-bye to my shipmates, and wobbled up towards the street. I was free, no longer shackled to the day-in, day-out machinations of sailing a 36-foot yacht through the relentless swells of the South Pacific. No longer a convict, of sorts, in a cruel form of punishment. I was a free man, able to do what I wanted, whenever I liked.

I piled my personal belongings into a taxi, and jockeyed my way through downtown Sydney, back to my sister's house in Bondi Beach, feeling—no surprise here—nauseous. I unpacked, and reclined on the sofa, letting out an enormous sigh of relief.

Then the phone rang. It was Geoff, and the Sydney-Mooloolabah Race (another well-known offshore event) was coming up. *Sweet Lauraine's* owner needed eight sailors who knew the boat well enough to race the vessel. Once again, my name had come up in a conversation among Sydney doctors. Once again, I committed to the adventure. And, a little bit like the Liberty Men of whom I'd grown so fond, my freedom was once again snatched up by the hungry jaws of the mighty South Pacific.

Inbreds in the Stream

(Bahamas, 2000)

"In humans about 42 percent of offspring from sister-brother marriages die before they reach reproductive age, hence most, though not all, cultures have strong traditions with respect to incest."
—From an introduction to university genetics course

"Packer [a research scientist] notes that female baboons appeared more careful to avoid inbreeding than males."
—Jim Moore, *Inbreeding and Outbreeding in Primates/The Natural History of Inbreeding and Outbreeding*

In early March 2000, the Burns Family Beach Fund was looking pretty skinny. It had spent much of winter on a liquidation diet and the ravages of paycheck-to-paycheck jobs had it whimpering in a corner of our local bank looking for crumbs. One day, I went to see the bank manager.

He assured me that while the account was still open, the fund within was on life support. If the fund were going to be of any use to anyone—which was the idea—it'd have to be fed carefully and nursed back to health.

"It might take six months; it might take a year," the bank manager warned me, "but it's possible that the fund can be revived."

Great news. But it was March. When you live near a ski resort, March is special. It's when you pool your nickels and try to afford a trip out. The beaches of Baja Mexico and the Caribbean, the reefs of Florida and Australia, the atolls of Tahiti and Bikini call those with the most nickels; Moab calls the rest of us. Luckily for my wife and me, (and unluckily for our hapless Beach Fund), Charlie French, an English friend from many adventures, had recently bought a yacht, the *Westwind*, and was living aboard ship. He suggested we murder the fund, buy a couple of plane tickets, and then meet him somewhere in Florida.

We took the advice, ignoring everything our parents ever told us about saving for a rainy day, and purchased two seats on a Continental jet. By March 19 we were out the door heading south and east.

Cruising—that subcategory of sailing which is so aptly named—is one of the finest leisure activities ever invented by man. Loading up a ship's worth of food, toys and diversions (which is a hell of a lot more than can fit in your average Winnebago) and hitting the sea for an extended period is the best holiday I think I've ever been involved with.

My wife Ann and I arrived at the Miami airport and wove our way through the crowded baggage claim area and out onto the street. Several taxis tried to flatten us while we were standing on the sidewalk next to a cop. "Welcome to Flawwda," the cop said, smiling. Luckily, Charlie arrived promptly and whisked us away in a rental car. We drove through mile after mile of urban sprawl in a heavy rain, stopping once at a liquor store to buy a 12-pack of cheap beer (my choice) and a couple of bottles of rare Australian wine (Charlie's choice).

We arrived at Marathon Key around midnight, and were introduced to Charlie's parents, Dorothy and Alan, and the boat itself. Charlie and Ann climbed aboard, then I. Alan studied me carefully as I tripped over the boat's wire railing. I dropped the suitcase I was carrying and fell down upon it. I picked myself up, and then tried to climb down inside the *Westwind.* My head bounced off a board covering the open hatch. I reeled and fell sideways on a couch. Alan leaned in through the opening and raised his eyebrows at me in a barely perceptible "I've-got-you-pegged-buddy" kind of manner.

"So, you've done some sailing, Charles tells us," he said.

"Oh yeah," I bragged, wiping the blood from my forehead. "Done some big off-shore races in Oz. You know, those round-the-clock events. Brutal stuff."

"Which ones?"

"The Hobart-to-Sydney?" I suggested.

"Hmmm … Isn't it called the Sydney-to-Hobart?" Alan asked.

"No, the Hobart-to-Sydney is a new version of the old Sydney-to-Hobart. It's much harder. You have to bring along non-sailors as part of the crew."

"Oh. It sounds incredibly … um, strange."

"It can be," I said, tearing open a side of the 12-pack we bought in Miami and opening a cold Budweiser. "Say, where should I put the beer?"

"Put it in the bow," Charlie called out. I wandered to the rear of the boat and dumped the beer out on a large bed, then went upstairs to look at the stars.

We set off from Marathon Key the next day and sailed the inner coastal regions of the Gulf of Florida, that shallow area squashed between the Florida Keys to the south and the mainland to the north. A small, brief rainstorm struck, but the wind was perfect and we enjoyed views of the Florida Keys that most Americans will never see. As night fell, we anchored off Key Largo, at the top end of the chain. Our heads were woozy, but the gentle rolling of the swells was also calming in a strange, tiring way. It was a good night. We needed soothing. On the morrow we'd face the Straits of Florida, and the dreaded Gulf Stream.

Most southerners are familiar with the Gulf Stream and most southern sailors are intimate with the legendary current, but to the average non-sailor it requires a brief introduction. In simple terms, the Gulf Stream is a small portion of a huge ocean current that traverses the North Atlantic Ocean (called—surprise, surprise—the North Atlantic Current), which is in turn part of a larger set of currents circling the globe.

Shallow, warm water from the Pacific and Southeast Asia flows west around the southern tip of Africa, then northwest, across the equator and past the eastern tip of Cuba. A large portion of this massive ocean current circles southwest around the Bahamas, runs the gap between the Bahamas and Florida, then continues north along North America's Atlantic Coast. Upon reaching the Saint Lawrence River in Canada, the current heads east, towards Great Britain and Northern Europe. It finally slows down in the Norwegian Sea where the water cools and sinks, then circles around Iceland and heads south. It follows the East Coast of Greenland, then, more or less, heads south down the middle of the Atlantic.

By the time this cool water reaches the Central North Atlantic, it has sunk to a much lower depth than the warm water heading north, and simply passes under it, like cars on a freeway on-ramp. From the Central North Atlantic, the current heads southeast again, back towards the Pacific. And the cycle repeats itself.

The Gulf Stream is probably the most unique part of this entire system. It is so warm, and so well-defined, that when viewed by temperature-sensitive devices from outer space, it looks like a bright orange streamer. The current is so powerful that scientists believe it causes London's fogs and is responsible for Northern Europe's moderate climate. Debris from sunken ships and bottled messages dropped in the Florida Straits are regularly found in Europe.

It's likely that the first European to be aware of this powerful current was the Spanish mariner Juan Ponce de Leon. During his 1513 explorations for the Fountain of Youth, Ponce de Leon traversed the Florida Straits. He had all his sails up, and there was a strong breeze blowing south, yet, for some reason, the boat moved backward (north) in the water—the current pushing him north was stronger than the wind pushing him south. He maneuvered his ship closer to the Florida coastline and once out of the current, continued happily on his way.

It wasn't until Benjamin Franklin, the great American statesman and scientist, began observing shipping between Boston and England that the northern effects of the Gulf Stream were better understood. Franklin, that most astute observer and inventor of bifocals and the lightning rod, sailed many times to Europe as a diplomat, and during his trips he noticed that ships sailing from Boston to England took two days less than ships sailing west across the Atlantic. He also noticed that ships took a different route in each direction. Sailors were obviously onto something, but how much they understood is difficult to know.

Franklin experimented, dropping objects into the sea and charting temperatures. Despite his crude instruments, he was able to describe the position of the current quite accurately. The great inventor and scientist was not correct, however, in his assumption that the current originated in the Gulf of Mexico.

Today, on nautical charts of the Caribbean, the Gulf Stream stands out like a giant vacuum. Dozens of arrows point north between Florida and the western edge of the Bahamas indicating the strength and speed of the water's force. It lies in wait, ready to suck tiny vessels out into the North Atlantic the way a busted window in an airplane sucks out human bodies. Get caught, and who knows where you'll go.

To our team of neophyte Gilligans, the charts were intriguing. We gazed wide-eyed at the arrows, and wondered which episode of Gilligan's many adventures we were going to relive.

Although Alan and Dorothy were well-seasoned in the sailing department, and a crew of three (Alan, Dorothy, Charlie) was adequate for a crossing of the Straits, Charlie had called me because he knew I'd done some real sailing. South Pacific stuff with the Roaring Forties thrown in. Dangerous Aussie surf. Big seas. Hard rain. Tough men. Blood, pain, and sweat. I'd assured Charlie I was his man. He'd taken the bait, and now, here I was—the Great Sailor ready for action, my wife backing me up all the way ("Cam's an expert sailor. His Dad has a Folbot in the basement."). I spent the entire night hiding in my bunk drinking beer, and pointedly avoiding the serious nautical chitchat that was taking place in the main cabin.

On the morning of March 21, we set off. The water was calm, the surface glassy. There was no wind. So, after 45 minutes of sitting doing nothing (which, because we weren't moving, actually felt like 45 minutes of sunburning our necks into potato-chip crispness), Charlie cranked up the *Westwind's* motor and we started motoring. As we putted along, we tried to figure out exactly where we were. Were we in the Stream yet? Or were we still on the coastal shelf? Suddenly, the water turned a deep, dark menacing blue. It was still glassy and calm, but the swells were bigger—big, glassy, smooth swells. We rolled gently up and down over the ocean, our slitted eyes scanning the horizon for tsunamis, waterspouts and hurricanes.

Strange objects—looking uncannily like garbage—went drifting past. Caught in the current, they were heading north at several knots. I saw several white plastic grocery bags, and pieces of an old-fashioned Styrofoam cooler go drifting by, undoubtedly bound for England. I pointed this out to Ann, "Look. Britain gave us our language and culture, and now were giving something back!"

Alan furrowed his brow.

As we progressed east, trepidation was overtaken by another emotion—a sort of growing resentment. Enormous, multimillion-dollar "yachts" (with no sails, and powered by aircraft engines the size of Tuff Sheds) buzzed past, churning the swells into creamy mashed potatoes. The resentment grew slightly as we rocked sideways.

These massive white yachts contained Florida's equivalent of the jet set. Well-heeled, martini-swilling middle-aged people with white hair and blotchy brown skin motored past, undoubtedly headed for Nassau's casinos and nightlife. They churned the water into foam and barely looked down at us real sailors as they chugged by. The most we ever got was a raise of the martini glass.

That was okay, I told myself. We were the real deal, tackling the Straits on the ocean's terms, a few tough men and a couple of brave women against powerful natural forces. In literary terms—man versus nature. Maybe there'd be a mutiny—man versus man. Perhaps one of us would go nuts—man versus himself. Any tough, real-life scenario was possible.

Unfortunately, the wind was nonexistent, so we had to kick up the *Westwind's* motor. I wished we'd had a bigger motor, so we could have raced the martini crowd. I sat back with a generic beer and watched the garbage floating to England, realizing for the first time that I had Tuff-Shed-Sized-Motor Envy.

Ten smooth, calm hours later, we spotted a few lone rocks jutting out of the water. One of these, South Riding Rock, is the southernmost outpost of the Bimini Islands group—Hemingway's famed *Islands in the Stream.* We aimed our soft hull for this spiky jab of land, and pretty soon the deep, dark blue trench that had been below us disappeared, in its place shallow, light blue waters. The Straits were behind us, and now we were above the Great Bahama Bank, a giant slab of limestone sitting just under the surface of the ocean.

The Bahamas are generally not considered part of the Caribbean islands. A quick look at a map shows why. The Bahamas—northeast of Cuba—are part of the North American tectonic plate, and do not border the Caribbean Sea, as do the real Caribbean islands, the Lesser Antilles, islands between Puerto Rico and South America, and Greater Antilles, Cuba, Hispaniola, Puerto Rica and Jamaica.

The Bahamas include some 700 islands and 2,500 islets, tiny, uninhabitable rocky outcrops barely rising out of the ocean, spread out across an area of roughly 100,000 square miles. The term cay, pronounced *key*, is an Anglicized Lucayan Indian word meaning small island from the Lucayan *cairi*. The names of islands in the Bahamas can be quite confusing. Some of the tiniest bumps of rock might be called island, while some of the larger islands have been dubbed cay. The confusion, apparently, is a result of the history—various visitors to the Bahamas gave their own names to islands, regardless of size.

More impressive than the number of islands, however, is this gigantic limestone block lying just under the surface of the water. Many geologists regard this limestone shelf—or bank—as the biggest piece of limestone in the world. It is estimated by some to be 20,000 feet thick. On its top side, the massive block is so uniform that almost everywhere one travels in the Bahamas the bottom of the ocean floor is no more than 50 feet down.

Oceanographers estimate that if sea level were 50 feet lower, the Bahamas would consist of just two islands: Great Bahama Bank and Little Bahama Bank. The present Bahamas would be mere hills on the two main islands. Captains of Spanish galleons were so impressed by the nature of Bahamian waters, they coined a term for the ocean here, *baja mar*, or shallow sea. Light reflected off the shallow ocean floor makes for fabulous snorkeling and swimming.

Over eons, geologic action has caused the division and erosion of the Bahamian banks. Deep gorges have formed between sections of the massive limestone banks, so that today the flat-topped underwater plateaus are separated by ocean trenches, called sounds and channels. The best name is applied to the biggest trench, the so-called Tongue of the Ocean, which carves its way through the middle of the Bahamas reaching depths of many thousands of feet.

According to several books I scanned, the Bahamas were first settled by a group of peaceful Indians called the Lucayans, *lukku-caire* or island people in Lucayan, who came from South America. The Lucayans were fleeing an aggressive group of cannibals, the Caribes. As they fled, the Lucayans migrated from one Caribbean island to another, until they eventually occupied the Bahamas. The Caribes never made it that far north, and the Lucayans were able to live in relative tranquility.

It was the Bahamas where Christopher Columbus first sighted the New World when he sailed west from Spain in 1492. It has been hotly debated for years as to which island he visited first: present-day San Salvador (the Bahamian island northeast of Rum Cay, not to be confused with the capital city of Central America's El Salvador) or Samana Cay, 60 miles southeast of present-day San Salvador. Interestingly, Samana Cay has also been historically known as San Salvador confusing matters infinitely, but keeping a few obscure historians (and bad travel writers) employed.

There are so many wonderful, surprising and bizarre aspects of the Bahamas that it's hard to know with which one to become obsessed. Now that we'd reached South Riding Rock at the southern end of the Bimini group, and the huge block of limestone, I knew which Bahamian Weirdthing would grab me hardest—the famed Lost Continent, Atlantis.

I'd wanted to conduct my own search for Atlantis for years, and now, bobbing in the tiny waves around South Riding Rock, I had my chance. My search would be a bit different from most, and would basically involve peering at the sea floor from the boat's deck. Sure, it wasn't scientific in the traditional understanding of *scientific,* but likely as accurate as any assessment of Atlantis to date.

The possible existence and location of Atlantis has been one of the great mysteries of the modern world and tens of thousands of individuals—from scientists and scholars to clairvoyants and mystics, who in this pursuit are labeled *Atlantologists*—have joined the search for the fabled civilization. Even Adolf Hitler supposedly searched for Atlantis. He believed his "Aryan" people were descended from the Atlanteans of legend—strong, superior, blond and flawless.

Somewhere between 2,000 and 10,000 books (no one knows for sure) have been written about Atlantis, and countless millions have been spent searching for the fabled land. It has become, in fact, a rather large industry.

All this Atlantis stuff started over 2,000 years ago when Plato wrote two stories called *Critias* and *Timeaus*, way back in 360 B.C. Both stories were named after real men who existed in Plato's day; they are the ones credited with telling the legend of Atlantis to Plato and others.

According to Plato, the stories Critias and Timeaus (the men) told originated with some Egyptian priests from a place called Sais. These priests told the stories to Solon (630-560 B.C.), a Greek ruler who visited Egypt around 590 BC. Solon, in turn, passed the stories along to a fellow named Dropides, who told his son Critias (a man), who passed the stories along to his grandson Critias (another man). The grandson Critias and his friend Timeaus, in turn, passed the stories *Critias* and *Timeaus* along to Socrates and Hermocrates. Confused?

The subsequent stories *Critias* and *Timeaus* were in response to a lecture by Socrates about ideal societies—Timeaus and Critias (the men) agree to entertain Socrates with a tale that is "not a fiction but a true story" about an ideal society. While Critias and Timeaus told the stories *Critias* and *Timeaus*, Plato wrote them down for all eternity.

Regardless of the mechanics of how Plato's stories originated (which is a great discussion in itself, and there are plenty of more mangled explanations than mine) Plato was the only ancient writer to ever mention Atlantis. All other references to the lost continent have been based upon his stories, begging the question: did Plato make this up?

I must ask: who really cares? After all, although Plato spawned a highly questionable, quasi-occult industry in the international search for Atlantis, it's pretty harmless and, at times, fairly entertaining. What other story has created an entirely new line of science (i.e., Atlantology)? Even pervasive legends of Bigfoot in the Western United States haven't produced Sasquatchology. How about Elvisology? I don't think so. Besides, Atlantology works perfectly for my brand of journalism.

The Atlantis Plato described in *Critias* and *Timeaus* existed some 9,000 years before Plato's time (428-347 B.C.), or roughly 11,400 years before our time. It was a lost island-continent, a lush place, with an abundance of natural resources and a superhuman race of people who peacefully ruled all the surrounding island states. It was located "outside the Pillars of Hercules" and "was an island greater in extent than Libya and Asia, and when afterwards sunk by an earthquake, became an impassable barrier of mud to voyagers sailing from hence to any part of the ocean."

To date, the strongest theories about where Atlantis was located have focused on various islands off the west coast of Africa, the Bahamas and Caribbean islands, the Greek island of Santorini (Thera), Crete, Peru, Bolivia, Mexico, Costa Rica, islands in the North Sea, and in Antarctica—in other words, the search area is not narrowing. Pretty much every place on earth where you find land and water is a candidate. Soon Atlantologists will be looking seriously at Mars.

Indeed, just recently, a fellow named Arysio Nunes dos Santos—a professor of nuclear physics at the Federal University of Minas Gerais, Brazil—has proposed that Atlantis was really the entire Indonesian-Malaysian chain of islands and archipelagoes, which 11,600 years ago formed something of a continent-sized wedge of land between Australia, China and Southeast Asia.

"The explosion of Mt. Krakatoa caused a giant tsunami, which ravaged the lowlands of Atlantis and Lemuria," Nunes dos Santos writes. "It also triggered the end of the Ice Age by covering the continental glaciers with a layer of soot which precipitated their melting by increasing the absorption of sunshine. The meltwaters of the glaciers flowed into the oceans, raising sea levels by about 100-150 meters and causing tremendous strains and stresses in the crust of the earth. This cracked open in the weak spots, engendering further volcanic eruptions and earthquakes that feedback (positively) the process, furthering it to completion. The result was the dramatic end of the Pleistocene Ice Age and the so-called Quaternary Extinctions which we mentioned above."

If you read any of the good professor's musings about Atlantis, you'll find he has some very plausible theories. (One has to wonder if nuclear physics students at the Federal University of Minas Gerais, Brazil, are receiving the scholarship they expected.) Unfortunately, in the spring of

2000, I didn't have the prerequisite nickels to go scuba diving in the South China Sea, so I had to be content with snorkeling in the Bahamas, where I concentrated my search. As Charlie, Alan, Dorothy, Ann and I floated across the southern end of the Bimini chunk of the Great Bahama Bank, I peered into the azure water. It was hard to see the bottom. Daylight was waning, and the boat was rocking. Remarkably, I could just make out some squarish-looking shapes under the water—stone blocks, big limestone blocks that looked like they were cut into perfect shapes by men, or aliens, or Mer People, or even nuclear physicists from Minas Gerais, Brazil.

It was stone blocks similar to these that caused something of a Bimini Subsidiary in the Worldwide Atlantis Search Business. In the early part of the 20th century, a fellow by the name of Edgar Cayce (1877-1945) described the discovery of Atlantis in an area just north of where I was now floating. Cayce (pronounced "Casey") was America's best-known psychic and clairvoyant while he was alive. "At the age of 21, he was stricken with a paralysis of the throat muscles and putting himself into an hypnotic sleep, he prescribed his own medication, which cured him," wrote Richard Ellis in his 1998 book *Imagining Atlantis*. "Cayce applied this technique to other patients: lying on his back with his feet facing north, he required only the name and address to be able to diagnose their disorders and recommend osteopathic and homeopathic cures."

Cayce could also "see" into history, and describe people, places and situations that had thus far been overlooked by conventional historians. Rather than write down his own observations, Cayce—who did all his prediction work in a trance—dictated his visions to various stenographers, who scribbled furiously while Cayce spoke. When Cayce died, he left a whopping 14,000 written statements, predictions and observations. Some of these predictions were about the search for Atlantis.

Specifically, Cayce predicted the Lost Continent would be found sometime in 1968 or '69, "between the Gulf of Mexico on the one hand and the Mediterranean on the other … there are some protruding portions … that must have been at one time or another a portion of this great continent. The British West Indies, or the Bahamas, are a portion of same that may be seen in the present. If the geological survey would be made in some of these, especially or notably in Bimini and the Gulf Stream through this vicinity, these may be even yet determined." (Clearly, Cayce had a few drunk stenographers in his employ.)

Edgar Cayce's techniques might've sounded slightly less scientific than my own endeavors aboard Charlie's boat, but they weren't lacking for research. His predication about the location of Atlantis came from "life readings" he did on some 1,600 people, 50 percent of whom had been reincarnated and had lived previous lives on Atlantis. (Hey, if you want to know about Atlantis, just ask the Atlanteans.) Anyway, no one knew for sure what to make of Cayce's predictions except, of course, to go look for the place. And "Atlantis" was eventually found—several dozen times.

In 1968, two commercial pilots, Capt. Robert Brush and his co-pilot Trigg Adams, spotted a strange, rectangular object in the shallow waters near Andros, the largest Bahamian island. Back in Miami, the two pilots reported their find to two friends, Dimitri Rebikoff and J. Manson Valentine. Rebikoff was a famed French oceanographer; Valentine, a zoologist and research associate of Honolulu's Bishop Museum. The two men—both followers of Edgar Cayce—made plans to investigate.

"It was subsequently determined that the rectangular structure was approximately 34-by-20 meters and had an east-west orientation" wrote Andrew Collins, author of *Gateway to Atlantis*. "It was marked out by a layer of sea-grass, under which were said to be perfectly laid limestone blocks about a meter thick. The structure was also divided by a further 'wall' at its eastern end."

In a statement to the press in August 1968, Valentine and Rebikoff told the world of the find, and described the object as an Atlantean temple. Of course, there was an international controversy about said temple, especially since it was later found to be a "sponge pen" (presumably a netted box-type device for gathering sea sponges). Regardless, more expeditions were mounted.

A quick look at any of the current web pages out there (several hundred thousand reference Atlantis) and you'll see that every man and his dog and his dog's Uncle Bob were out there looking for Atlantis, and that they still are today. Expedition leaders were reporting everything: buildings, roads, aqueducts, temples, statues, canals, cities—even a column "that radiated energy and blinking lights" to a 650-foot-tall underwater pyramid, with "sparkling white water flowing out of the openings in the pyramid and surrounded by green water, instead of the black water everywhere else at that depth."

The most famous find though, was the Bimini Road, a series of rectangular stones laid out along an axis for several hundred feet, and, honestly, looking as much like part of a city as anything else out there. (Geologists say the road is nothing more than a stone called beach rock which fractures into perfect corners.)

I think the expedition that Cayce would have liked the most was a 1968 "search" by Robert Ferro and Michael Grumley of New Jersey. After their experience, they wrote a book called *Atlantis: The Autobiography of a Search: A Psychic and Real Journey to Find the Lost Continent as Prophesied by Edgar Cayce.*

Ellis sums up the Ferro-Grumley expedition succinctly in *Imagining Atlantis*: "There are too many books about the lost continent to discuss more than a select few, but Ferro and Grumley's is particularly interesting because, by the authors' own admission, they were under the influence of Tarot readers and marijuana (which they wrote 'is a key which could unlock certainly previously closed doorways of perception') and the Cayce Institute in Virginia Beach. Thus equipped, they could hardly fail to find the Lost Continent, and in the warm, clear waters of Bimini, they encountered a geometrical pattern of rectangular rocks that they identified as 'proof of an ancient civilization that may have been Atlantis'."

The sheer number of Atlantis expeditions to the Bahamas is astonishing, but if you think about it, not at all surprising. Going floating around in some of the warmest, bluest, most beautiful seawater on earth is a pretty easy sell. Snorkeling and scuba diving in these waters makes it even more appealing.

My own expedition to Bimini (or rather to South Riding Rock, which is a long way south of Bimini and bares virtually no relationship to the Bimini Road) was in the classic Ferro-Grumley style. We came, we swam, we looked at the clear blue water and saw all sorts of weird and wonderful sights, even without the marijuana.

After leaving Riding Rock, we struck out across the great limestone shelf, watching the ocean floor a few feet below our boat. I was secretly hoping to find a temple, a stone, carving or perhaps even some Atlantean coins. After a while, I became bored with staring at the sea floor and tried my hand at fishing, only to snag a giant green garbage bag (empty), which required a hell of a lot of energy to land.

We moored a second night off Chub Cay, a tiny island used by most sailors for refueling when traveling between Florida and Nassau. Chub Cay is a small, quiet and very personable island. There's not much going on, but heck, who would want to be here if there was? A cluster of several dozen gigantic houses dominates the town, and look wildly out-of-place on a Bahamian island. According to the Lonely Planet guide to the Bahamas,

Quincy Jones has a house on Chub Cay.

While we were refueling, I studied the map. The Bahamas cover such a large area, and the sea floor is so shallow, that it's not hard imagining that the entire limestone block was once a continent. As I noted earlier, if the world's oceans were just a few feet shallower, the entire block would be above water. This fact has prompted many Atlantologists to delve further into Plato's numbers, specifically, the measurements he gives for Atlantis in *Critias*.

Plato's measurements are in stadias, the old Greek measurement from which our modern sports stadiums get their size. *Webster's Revised Unabridged Dictionary* (1913), which I just happen to have lying next to my keyboard, describes a stadia as "a Greek measure of length, being the chief one used for itinerary distances, also adopted by the Romans for nautical and astronomical measurements." One stadia was equal, according to Mr. Webster, to "606 feet nine inches English."

Anyway, when you start counting your stadias, and measure the size of the Great Bahama Bank—which runs from the Bimini and Berry Islands down through Andros to Long Island and really is shaped in the complex way Plato described Atlantis—some interesting similarities occur. For example, Plato wrote that Atlantis was 3,000 stadia long, 2,000 stadia wide, "of an oblong shape," and "... away from the rest of the continent, while the surrounding basin of the sea is everywhere deep in the neighborhood of the shore ...," which, it turns out, is a pretty good description of the Great Bahama Bank.

Further, Plato wrote that "the whole country was said by him to be very lofty and precipitous on the side of the sea ..." which the Great Bahama Bank is; that it was "smooth and even," which it is; and that Atlantis "... became an impassable barrier of mud to voyagers sailing from hence to any part of the ocean ..." which is true, if you figure people were traveling to and from anywhere near Central America to other parts of the world.

Even Plato's comment "There were a great number of elephants in the island ... [of Atlantis]" can be explained by reasoning that, at the time, 11,600 years ago, mastodons and mammoths could be found all over North America.

We kept sailing.

After leaving Chub Cay, one strikes out across a gigantic trench that slices through the middle of the Great Bahama Bank like an oceanic Grand Canyon. It's called, appropriately, the Tongue of the Ocean. Like the Florida Straits, the Tongue is an utter trench. According to the literature, it is estimated to plunge some 5,000-6,000 feet into the earth, to depths guys like me with cheap snorkeling gear will likely never go. It is dark and blue to the eye, and slightly cold to the touch. When you're sailing along over light blue *baja mar* and suddenly drift out of the Tongue of the Ocean, your stomach does a somersault. It doesn't matter that you're just as safe as you were where the sea is 50 feet deep, it's that it is so incredibly dark and foreboding and scary. If there are monsters in the world's oceans, this is where they'll be.

And the name is so colorful, it makes you wonder. I'd like to think it was named because your tongue drops out of your head when you look down, but alas, it was likely named because it really is tongue-shaped. It comes snaking its way into the limestone block of the Great Bahama Bank, licking at the edges of the Berry Islands and New Providence.

Interestingly, this gigantic trench fits in somewhat with the description of Atlantis Plato left us: "And beginning from the sea they bored a canal of three hundred feet in width and one hundred feet in depth and fifty stadia in length, which they carried through to the outermost zone, making a passage from the sea up to this, which became a harbor, and leaving an opening sufficient to enable the largest vessels to find ingress."

Later, in describing "the channel which led to the sea," Plato wrote "The entire area was densely crowded with habitations; and the canal and the largest of the harbours were full of vessels and merchants coming from all parts, who, from their numbers, kept up a multitudinous sound of human voices, and din and clatter of all sorts night and day." To me, these canals sounded much like the trenches that cut through the Great Bahama Bank: the Tongue, the New Providence Channel, and other deep gorges that—as I said—would have been perfect harbors if the sea were 50 feet lower.

It seemed an interesting theory, and one which to my knowledge hasn't been explored. Problem is, you'd have to dive way, way, way down into the Tongue or New Providence Channel to find the sunken Atlantean ships, which probably meant some new, really expensive snorkeling gear, and I was broke. We carried on, with the Tongue lapping at the hull of the *Westwind* all the way to Nassau.

Nassau, the Bahamian capital, lies on a tiny island called New Providence. While most of the Bahamas are virtually uninhabited, two-thirds of the country's population lives on New Providence. The island's importance came about for two basic reasons. In the mid-17th century, the British sailors and colonizers found that the north side of New Providence had possibly the best harbor in the Bahamas, Nassau Harbour. This natural port lies between New Providence and Paradise Island just a half-mile to the north, is well protected from the ocean's vagaries, and is also comparatively deep.

The other reason is New Providence's central location in the entire Bahamian group, from which the British government could administer most of its Bahamian territory. The British erected various forts and colonial buildings, and weathered several skirmishes with Spanish and French warships at the turn of the 18th century.

These days, Nassau is like a cross between South Central Los Angeles and Las Vegas. The city of 180,000 boasts a pretty solid crime rate, while on its northern flank sits Paradise Island, a booming Vegas-like Disneyland with a massive casino/marina/hideous monstrosity called (what else?) Atlantis.

Of course, stepping off the boat onto one of Nassau's marinas made us feel landsick. We'd just gotten used to the constant rolling of the ocean, so when it abruptly stopped, I was ready for a bucket. We dined at a popular establishment called the Poop Deck, then retired to the *Westwind* for sleep. In the morning, we bid farewell to Alan and Dorothy, who were headed back to England and the rain and the wonderfully diverse garbage floating up from Florida. Charlie took them to the airport, then we set sail again. Destination: Eleuthera and Spanish Wells.

Eleuthera is a long stretch of limestone standing as a massive natural barrier between the raging North Atlantic and the calmer *baja mar*. En route to it, we decided we should examine Current Cut, a thin drainage between two 20-mile-long islands. Here, tidal currents force ocean water through the tiny gap at speeds of about eight knots and sailing manuals for the Bahamas warn that it is best to travel through the cut during slack tide (which I learned was when it's high or low, not going in or out). We arrived while the cut was going in (or maybe out—who could tell). Anyway, it was pushing millions of gallons of water our direction. We bided our time until slack tide by snorkeling under the boat and studying a massive barracuda who had little fear of humans.

Once through the cut, we tacked north to Spanish Wells, a tiny town perched on the northern edge of St. George's Island, a subsidiary island just east of Eleuthera. Spanish Wells (population 800) was a delightful place. The streets were small and neat, the people friendly and the houses colorful. A gentle breeze blew constantly off the Northeast Providence Channel, and the smell of the ocean on the wind was intoxicating. Charlie parked the *Westwind* at the local Marina, and we wandered into the village to buy groceries. On the way back to the boat, a local woman gave us a ride in her golf cart, one of the three most common modes of transportation on the island (the others being bicycles and scooters). We liked Spanish Wells so much, that we decided to stay a few nights.

The town was named because during the days of the Spanish exploration of the Americas, Spanish galleons would stop at St. George's Island to fill up on freshwater from the island's natural springs. The town itself dates back a long way. It is one of the first English settlements in the Bahamas, and—like most of the New World—it owes its history to the intolerance of English religions in the early 17th century.

At that time, the Anglican Church and Puritans were battling for control of England in a civil war. Many Puritans fled England and struck out to the New World, hoping to find tolerance in a new land. One group of settlers, under the leadership of Puritan Governor William Sayle, staked its claim in Bermuda. Unfortunately, intolerance was quick to follow, and in 1648, Sayle and about 70 others set out to found their own colony. Calling themselves the Company of Adventurers for the Plantation of the Islands of Eleuthera (Greek for freedom) they made it to the Abacos, but a rift between company members prompted the majority to head south, toward the island of Cigatoo, which they renamed Eleuthera.

Shortly before landing on Eleuthera, the Adventurers' boat struck the notorious Devil's Backbone, a maze of rocky spikes just below sea level off the north coast of Eleuthera, famed for its ability to rip boats to bits. The Adventurers managed to make it ashore, and holed up in a cave.

Sayle headed off by rowboat to gather support for his new colony, and eventually made it to Jamestown, Virginia. Jamestown residents apparently liked the idea of another colony based upon ideals of tolerance, and supplied the marooned Adventurers with provisions. Thus, the English were established in the Bahamas, and, some time thereafter, the English-founded Spanish Wells came into existence.

Within a few hours of landing, Charlie, Ann and I had wandered around most of the bustling metropolis of Spanish Wells, and were impressed with the cleanliness of the place, as well as the friendliness of the locals. We visited Pinder's Bakery and bought cake; Pinder's Supermarket, where we bought meats and vegetables, and wandered past Pinder's Garage, where several thin bony men were working on a tire.

As our first full day on the island progressed, something started bugging me. I couldn't quite put my finger on it—like a dull itch or a pebble in your shoe. While we trod the immaculate streets of Spanish Wells, gathering groceries for our next few days of sailing, all three of us were lost deep in thought. A female cyclist turned onto the street we were on, and headed towards us. We watched her pedal slowly past. Suddenly, Charlie broke the silence: "Hey, I saw that woman on the other side of town a minute ago," he said, scratching his head. "On a scooter. Now, there she goes on a bike!"

"That's strange," I added. "She sold us the groceries we just bought, and was wearing a pink dress. Now she's wearing a T-shirt and red pants. And see that man over there in the black shorts playing tennis? I just saw him wearing greasy black coveralls and working at the gas station."

Something really strange was going on. We stood in the middle of the quiet street, looking around. Several children wandered past, clutching schoolbooks.

"Well, let's get back to the boat and start dinner," I suggested.

As we tromped along the tarmac, a woman in a golf cart pulled alongside. She called something to us.

Unaware, I thought she was offering us some kind of taxi service, so I asked her to pull over. She did, and before I could even ask her how much it would cost to take us back to the Spanish Wells Marina, my stomach jumped. It was the same woman who had ridden past us on the bicycle.

"Weren't you just on a bicycle a minute ago?" I asked.

"No," she said. "Not me."

"Hmmm. Well, how much back to the marina?"

"How much for what?"

"A ride back to the marina."

"I don't know," she said.

"You are a taxi of some sort, right?" I asked.

"No. I thought you had waved at me," she said, "so I pulled over to see what you wanted."

"Oh." I pulled my groceries off her front seat. "Whoops."

"But, if you like, I'll give you a ride."

Ann, Charlie and I looked at each other, then piled into the little cart. A few minutes later we were back at the marina.

"Thanks!" I said jumping down.

Back in the *Westwind*, we dove into the research, which consisted of thumbing through the three books in our ship's library (two of which had titles like *Atlantic Fish That'll Kill You In Two Seconds or Less*, and *The Mariners Guide to Nautical Hand Flag Signals for the Outer Westwind Islands and Turaco*). We found the reference we were looking for, deep in the bowels of the Lonely Planet guide to the Bahamas: "The village [Spanish Wells] dates back of the days of Eleutheran Adventurers," the book stated. "This deeply religious, somewhat reticent, lily-white population follows a Mid-Western U.S. lifestyle, with a surprising level of sophistication, side-by-side with Swiss clean orderliness and undaunted quaintness. Intriguingly, generations of isolation have concentrated the gene pool, reflected in prevalent inbred traits. Half the island is named Pinder."

Can you say *Deliverance*? No wonder everyone in town had a massive overbite and spoke as though their mouths were full of marbles.

Even in this modern age, with cheap airline travel, sperm banks, FedEx, and a truly global community, inbreeding has remained a serious problem for some cultures isolated from fresh genetic stock. Iceland, in particular, shows some interesting genetic traits which are being studied by researchers. There, the gene pool has concentrated itself while at the same time, Icelanders have kept detailed records of family histories making gene studies more accurate than in other places.

"Inbreeding results from the mating of related individuals," wrote researcher B.G. Cassell, in a paper on the results of inbreeding in cattle (about the only paper I could easily find describing how this stuff works). "Generally, inbreds are less productive, less thrifty, and less fertile than non-inbred cattle."

It was the great evolution expert Charles Darwin who woke the world up to inbreeding with his 1876 book *The Effects of Cross- and Self-Fertilization in the Vegetable Kingdom*. Darwin experimented with 57 species of plants and found that inbreeding depression is not only one of evolution's most powerful forces, but that it is widespread in many plant communities.

In Spanish Wells, the residents know about the inbreeding problems, but there's probably little they can do. Most people who come to the island are visitors who don't stay long, and those that do stay are generally retirees from the States; not the kind of people who are interested in diversifying the gene pool. So, they're probably stuck with the overbites and marblemouths for a while, at least until the population goes through a major flux of some kind, which doesn't appear likely anytime soon.

Despite their physical traits, the Bahamians of Spanish Wells are some of the wealthiest citizens of the country. Spanish Wells is home to one of the world's most productive lobstering communities, and during the lobstering season all the men head to sea for months at a time. Individual families have their own secret lobstering spots and information about the areas are tightly kept family secrets, only spoken of when passed on from generation to generation. They are also some of the nicest Bahamians, welcoming all who want to see their small chunk of the world.

After a couple of days with the Pinders, it was time to visit Eleuthera Island. Eleuthera seemed to be the most geologically interesting of the Bahamas, a massive wall of limestone blocking the rolling North Atlantic from the tranquil *baja mar*.

Charlie and I were eager to check out the sea-cliff climbing potential on the island, and had brought along piles of ropes and other gear. Unfortunately, our impromptu Spanish Wells Genetics Study had taken too long, and we arrived on Eleuthera's west coasts on our next to last day. We came ashore, and—as the afternoon light slipped into night—found what looked like some of the best sea-cliff climbing in the Americas. Certainly, the bouldering was phenomenal.

Eleuthera is also one of the islands first and hardest hit by any hurricanes that come swirling off the equator. The island's sole road had ten-foot deep gouges through it in every direction, and the local motorists who drove it did so with trepidation. We wandered along the coast, looking at the phenomenal cliffs and dreaming of the climbs that could've been … At least we had some potentially saleable data from the Spanish Wells Genetics Study.

As we jetted back to Miami, from Nassau over the Berry Islands and Andros, over the Biminis and Riding Rock, I had time between bouts of airsickness to ponder the myth of Atlantis, and put all the stories, research material and concepts I'd absorbed into perspective. And like all good Atlantologists, I believe I have figured it out.

It is my firm belief—based upon my own meticulously gathered evidence—that the Pinders of Spanish Wells were the original Atlanteans. First of all, I must point out I have no scientific evidence on which to base this claim. Science is often overrated. As we all know, people have used "scientific" numbers for every argument and counterargument ever made, sometimes the same numbers supporting opposite sides.

What I have is a hunch. You know, the basis of all good television detective work. (Not to be confused with a lumpy back.) And in every single television show I've ever seen (100 percent, scientifically speaking now), when the detective has a hunch, he's right.

I doubt this will satisfy the world's scientists, but heck, just look at the evidence: the Atlanteans were described as people "who dwelt outside the Pillars of Hercules," they were described as having a great system of government set up, and they knew the sea. Hey, for a lumpy theory, the Pinders will do just fine.

Atlantis Schmatlantis, I say. It's all Greek to me.

THE ANIMAL KINGDOM

Perro Café: Experiments in Canine Cuisine, Yucatan-Style

(Mexico, 1998)

"Sufficient water for processing, chicken, beef, turkey, wheat gluten, whole rice, animal liver, meat byproducts, corn starch - modified, wheat flour, salt, potassium chloride, caramel color, tricalcium phosphate, sodium tripolphosphate, natural flavor, iron oxide, zinc sulfate, choline chloride, vitamin supplements (E, A, B12, D3), ferrous sulfate, copper sulfate, thiamin mononitrate (Vitamin B1), manganese sulfate, niacin, calcium pantothenate, riboflavin supplement (Vitamin B2), pyridoxine hydrochloride (Vitamin B6), potassium iodide, folic acid, sodium selenite, biotin."

—Ingredients listed on the back of a can of Alpo

"Highly Digestible!"

—Encouragement printed on the front of a can of Alpo

In 1998, I became a chef. Not just any kind of chef, mind you, but a chef for dogs and cats. It's not that my food was so bad that the only beings who would eat it were dogs and cats. Indeed, my creations were intended for dogs and cats. It all started when we were carrying cat litter and dog food home from our local supermarket, and happened to walk by a travel agent's office.

"South Pacific from $699," said one sign in the window.

"Fiji, Rotarua, Raratonga," said another.

"Tahiti—$800. Includes air," said a third.

I stopped to study the signs. My wife Ann stopped beside me.

"Air included," I said. "What about food and water?"

"Airfare, you knucklehead," Ann said.

"You sure?"

"Yes. Look."

Ann's finger indicated some fine print, which stated: "Airfare, plus seven nights/eight days accommodations, all meals and inter-island transportation. $800."

"For a Tahiti vacation!" I exclaimed. "That's amazing! Airfare to

Sydney usually runs $900 to $1,100 for the flight alone. We should look into it."

"You know me," Ann said. "I'm always up for the beach."

We pulled the door open and walked into the sprawling, air-conditioned office. A woman named Marilyn introduced herself and we sat down in two large, soft armchairs facing her desk. I placed the cat litter on the floor and the dog food in my lap.

Marilyn asked what we were interested in and we told her Tahiti. Apparently, Tahiti had been sucked into the same economic slump that had bedeviled much of Southeast Asia during early 1998, after a crash in the Japanese stock market caused by an overvaluation of Japanese real estate (although others blamed it on the devaluation of the Thai bhat). Some observers had already nicknamed it the Asian Flu.

Flu or no flu, it didn't matter to me. Tahiti was cheap, and I'd always wanted to go. Marilyn booked us a one-week trip to Moorea, a small island in French Polynesia, through a company called Tahiti Vacations. She never once mentioned how hungry the dogs of Playa del Carmen, Quintana Roo, Mexico, might be.

Thus, in mid-April, brimming with excitement and anticipation, we boarded a Los Angeles-to-Papeete flight on a French airline called AOM (Agence Ouvert à la Mer, or some such name that six years of high school French couldn't quite decipher). We crushed our bodies into square, coffin-like seats that had no rival on any airplane, anywhere in the world, and after a back-busting, butt-numbing eight hours, we awoke to feel a shudder as our plane banked into the final turn for Papeete's Faaa Airport.

The water was a deep blue. The mountains sprang from the islands as majestic green spires. The beaches were small and personal. Tahiti was going to be a week of pure paradise. We uncoiled from the seats and hammered our joints back into place with the heels of our hands. Then, we were led toward a line of French customs agents, who processed everyone—including the nervous Osama bin Laden-looking types in front of us—without a hitch. But when I stepped up to the customs desk, handed the stern gendarme my passport and smiled politely, our little hiatus in the lush South Pacific was brought to a screeching halt. My wife was allowed into Tahiti, she being a U.S. citizen and all, and I was not.

I am, as you would probably never guess, a citizen of Australia. I've lived in the U.S. for a couple of deacdes and have a resident alien or green card (which is colored white). And, as we were to learn in the weeks and months that followed, I am a citizen of a nation that had recently been dumping French wine out in the streets of Sydney in protest of France's nuclear testing in the South Pacific.

"Hey," my dear and all-too-Australian father told me in a conversation a few days after I was rejected from Faaa Airport, "didn't you hear? They recently burned down the French embassy in Perth." (Thanks, Dad. Where were you when we were planning this trip?)

I was politely shuffled into a small, ugly, dirty office, inhabited by dozens of sweating French policemen and customs agents where I was to wait until the next flight back to Los Angeles. I pled for salvation. I explained that in America, Australian politics went virtually unnoticed by U.S. news media. Watching CNN, how could one possibly know what was happening other than in Washington? I forced an innocent smile. Reconciliation would be a smart move.

"Pourquoi pas?" I asked in my best Parisian. "Dans tout les autres nations, c'est possible acquirer un visa quand on entrer cette nation."

The entire office stopped cold. No one moved. Every single gendarme turned to face me. They gazed straight into my eyes, emotionless. There was absolute silence. I looked around the room and waited. Nothing but vacant stares. Uh-oh. Now I'd done it. If my citizenship hadn't destroyed Franco-Australian relations, my complete buggery of the French language had. I let my head sink into my chest and gazed at the dirty linoleum floor. Finally, the nicest of the gendarmes—who'd been treating me pretty well up to this point—coughed, and moved toward the counter where I stood.

"I em zorry, Monsieur," he said in his thick Gaulish. "We cannot ah-low Australeins eento Frensh Polyneesia today."

Twenty minutes later, my wife and I were loaded into the next plane heading back to Los Angeles.

Late that night, in a hotel in Inglewood, California, I went to sleep, praying for a better day on the morrow. It came, and I made some fast calls to Marilyn begging her to get my wife and me to a beach, anywhere, immediately. Marital bliss would become a kick in the twins, I told her, if she didn't hurry. Ann had been wanting to spend a spring week on the ocean for the past five years. In my cunning, I'd talked her out of it every time, by convincing her that adventurous road trips throughout the Western U.S. were a far better expenditure of time and cash. Nineteen ninety-eight was to be her year. We'd be sifting sand between our toes somewhere, or else.

Marilyn came through, and within 20 minutes of waking up that day, my wife and I were inside a taxi bound for the Mexicana desk at LAX.

We hopped on a four-hour flight to Cancun, and counted our blessings. The beach was not far away. We immediately found a cab that would take us to Playa del Carmen, a quiet beach that stands in complete contrast to the obnoxious resorts of Cancun and Cozumel.

In Playa, we booked a cheap beachside room at a local institution, the Blue Parrot Hotel. Within a few hours, we were out strolling along the beach, sun in our eyes, wind in our hair, and most importantly, grains of sand sifting delightfully between our toes.

It didn't take too much strolling and sifting before we noticed that there were a lot of dogs in Playa del Carmen. Dozens and dozens of the things. Everywhere. Big dogs, little dogs, thin dogs, fat dogs, dogs with strong bodies, dogs with limps and injuries, dogs with healthy coats, and dogs with mange. We first noticed the dogs at the south end of town, down near a dock, where the ferry to Cozumel departed every couple of hours or so. There, the Hounds of Playa del Carmen congregated on the sand, in an area that wasn't being used by people, a spot where the dogs could sit, sleep and hang out with each other and not be hassled by any humans who might want them out of the way.

These dogs, we observed, exhibited amazing social sensibilities in that they knew what not to do. They knew not to bark and fight, not to chase cats through the streets, not to beg food from the locals, not to poop in the streets, and not to sniff the tourists' crotches. Their happy, calm, well-ordered existence seemed a model for all creatures that live in man's domain. In short, these dogs were smart.

At the beachside bar that night, one of the healthier-looking mutts we'd seen near the dock roamed past several times, stopping here and there to wag his tail and have his ears scratched by tourists. A young Mexican waiter, Wilberth, explained to us that that particular dog was named Silver, and that he had formerly belonged to the bar's manager. Silver, apparently tired with having a master, had taken to a life of living on the beach. Wilberth called Silver over, and introduced us.

How Silver ever got his name is a mystery. He was a medium-sized, light brown dog that appeared to be a cross between a boxer and a Labrador. The only thing I could ever guess was that the bar manager had thought silver meant brown, or something dog-related, in English.
Despite our fears of mange, rabies, gout, gall-bladder infections and whatever else this friendly pooch might've been harboring, Ann and I tentatively scratched his ears. He wagged his tail, and gave us a coy, submissive look. You know, the butter-melting kind. We were in love, and we spent

the rest of the evening alternating between petting Silver and running to the nearby bathroom to wash our hands. Of course, when we decided to turn in, Silver followed us back to our beachfront bungalow. He slept on the porch that night, and wagged his tail maniacally when we arose the next morning.

We wandered the streets and beaches of Playa del Carmen for the next few days, and everywhere we went, Silver tagged along. When we went into a café for breakfast, Silver would sneak in and sit underneath our table. When we ventured into a shop selling souvenirs and Mexican trinkets, Silver would wait patiently just outside the front door. And when we snorkeled in the cool, azure Caribbean, Silver would carefully guard our belongings on the beach.

About midway through our beach week, I decided I should offer Silver some food, so I trekked to the nearest grocery store for a couple of cans of dog food. That evening, as we enjoyed sunset from our beachside verandah, I emptied a can of Alpo into a dish and set it down. Silver sniffed, licked and tasted the food. Then, tentatively, he took a few bites. After finishing only a third of the proffered meal, Silver returned to his nook under one of the beach chairs. Silver, obviously, wasn't hungry. He was, we surmised, well-fed by all the local restaurant owners in Playa, who knew the animal affectionately.

The evening drifted into night, and my wife and I curled up in the beach chairs reading cheesy novels. Then, another dog came wandering up the beach. This dog, a black and healthy-looking male, smelled the Alpo and wandered over. He sniffed and licked Silver in a sort of doggie greeting, and then set to work finishing up what was left of Silver's dinner. The black dog seemed extremely hungry, so I opened the second can of Alpo. He polished that off, then wagged his tail as if asking for more. Having none, I hiked off to the grocery store—Silver in tow—and purchased five more cans of Alpo. When Silver and I returned, the black male had gone but a very timid black female, who obviously had a litter of pups stashed somewhere judging by her sagging teats, was licking the dish. She ran off when she saw Silver and me coming.

I loaded up the dish with three cans of dog food and went into the bungalow. When I peeked out the window, the small

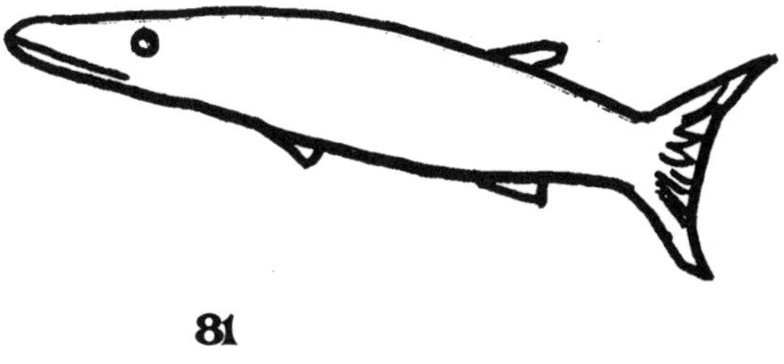

black female was chomping down the entire meal. Silver sat quietly nearby, watching her eat. The night drifted by, and dogs of all shapes and sizes wandered up to our porch, eating if they were hungry, and greeting Silver with licks, sniffs and wagging tails. Perro Café was born.

The next day, as Ann and I passed the grocery store, I bought 15 cans of Alpo. I explained in broken Spanglish to the curious clerk that all the dog food was "Para los perros a la Playa." We returned to our bungalow around five p.m., and I immediately set out the old dish with Alpo, and found three more plates which I loaded down with two cans of Alpo apiece.

"Perro Café is now open, huh?" my wife said, shaking her head in both wonder and disbelief. "What's on the menu tonight? Any specials?"

Admittedly, she had a point. The menu was rather bland. My Bifsteks de Alpo, Alpo Loaf and Alpo à la Mode were all pretty much the same thing: a pile of cheap dog food on a plate. But what Perro Café lacked in culinary delights, Silver and I made up for in atmosphere. We placed water bowls around the periphery of the verandah, within easy reach of the clientele, and even took a couple of bowls of dog food down a nearby side alley for the more timid dogs and cats of Playa del Carmen. We turned off the music inside the bungalow, and set the exterior lights down so that passing dogs could see Silver sitting happily near the front of the bungalow but not be frightened away by us humans. I even barked at passers-by on the beach, to let them know the café was open.

The night was a resounding success for Playa del Carmen's newest dining establishment. Fifteen dogs and five cats were served, and there was not a scrap of dog food left. Silver and I celebrated by ordering a plate of

ribs at the hotel restaurant, and shared the entire meal on a lounge chair on the beach. That we didn't actually turn a profit on the café didn't matter to Silver and me—no one was keeping the books anyway.

I've always been a pet lover. Cats, dogs, horses, ducks, sheep, rabbits, cows, you name it. I was lucky enough to grow up in the rural outskirts of Sydney (which are no longer rural and shouldn't be called outskirts anyway—*sprawlie edges* is a better term) and animals were just part of everyday life. Sharing life with animals—tame or wild—always seemed to me to be one of life's greatest joys.

Throughout my travels, I've had the good fortune to see how various world societies relate to their pets. Some are good, some not so good. Mexico is often regarded by those of us living north of the border as a place where domesticated animals are treated poorly. Sure, in the shantytowns around Mexico City it's not uncommon to see hundreds of mangy dogs and cats, many so skinny and sick (and lactating from recent litters) it's remarkable they're still alive. But before we condemn a country like Mexico for poor animal ethics, it's important to ask whether we're doing much better?

Aspen, Colorado, where I lived for four years, is regarded by many as a pretty sophisticated town. But some of the ways in which dogs and cats are treated by this sophisticated society surprised me, once I heard about them.

Seth "Dog Boy" Sachson owns the Aspen Boarding Kennel and Shelter, a tiny concrete building in Aspen's Airport Business Center, a sort of light-industrial complex on the outskirts of town. At the beginning and end of each ski season, dozens of dogs and cats are brought to Seth's shelter. The people getting rid of these pets are often young ski-area workers, and the main reason they abandon pets is Aspen's tough housing market. Many landlords don't allow tenants to have animals because of a few destructive habits, so for a typical ski bum to find an apartment or room where they can keep a dog or cat is nearly impossible. Divorce and animal behavioral problems follow as secondary and tertiary reasons animals are left at the shelter. Regardless of the reasons for getting rid of a pet, the methods can be cruel.

"I arrived one morning to find a pregnant pit bull terrier tied to the front door of the shelter," Seth said. "She was incredibly friendly, and we bonded for about two weeks before she had her puppies. She ignored the first puppy and left it lying in the sac, suffocating, motherless, dying. I broke the sac, cleared the fluid and placed the puppy against her teats. All was well. A total of eight healthy puppies were born, and they are now thriving in different homes around Aspen.

"One guy dropped off a dog that he claimed to have found running on the highway. We took it in, but he came back an hour later crying and apologizing for having lied to us. In the hour away from his dog, the man realized how much he loved him and did not want to give him up due to housing problems. He vowed to find new housing and remain committed to his dog. We released the dog back to the man.

"The worst is what I call the 'Puppy Mill Phenomenon,'" he said. "Even though the term here is technically incorrect, it describes the attitude. Many people do let their dogs have puppies so that the children can experience 'the miracle of birth' or so that their dog can 'have the experience of being a mother.'"

Dog Boy Seth often has to deal with the time, expense, extra workload and stress created by these "miracle of lifers" when they decide to deposit their unwanted litters at his shelter.

"We're talking about some pretty irresponsible actions in today's world with so many homeless pets that are euthanized, abandoned or simply dropped off at shelters like mine," he said.

In the late 1990s, Colorado State University veterinary epidemiologist Dr. M.D. Salman conducted two studies on how Americans treat domestic animals, particularly cats and dogs. Salman and his team found that of the roughly 1,000 animal shelters nationwide that responded to a survey, roughly four million pets were deposited at these shelters each year from 1994 to 1996 (To be clear, that adds up to 12 million pets for that period from the 1,000 shelters that responded. No one knows how many shelters there are altogether.)

"Of those sent to the reporting shelters that participated in the study, about 64 percent—or 8.2 million pets—were euthanized," according to a statement describing the study. "The survey also revealed that, on average, 42.5 percent of pets that entered animal shelters were submitted by animal control authorities and nearly 30 percent were surrendered by owners. The remainder were relinquished by other sources. Twenty-four percent, or three million, of the animals taken to shelters over the three-year period were adopted by new families. Only ten percent, or 1.2 million, were reclaimed by their owners."

Total euthanasia numbers in the United States are hard to come by (I've read that the officials estimates are around 25 million pets per year), but if you look at even a few studies, it would appear we're killing off our animals much more quickly.

A group called Second Chance Dogs did a study on the number of dogs euthanized at 19 Atlanta-area pet shelters and found that in 1998 alone 86,000 dogs had been "put down." Also, in 1998, it was estimated that at Rappanock, Virgina, area shelters, 6,128 "companion" animals were "abandoned and terminated." (According to the U.S. Census Bureau, Rappanock County had about 7,000 residents in 2000.) A recent estimate for the number of cats euthanized in Los Angeles annually put the total at four million. Although these numbers are mere estimates (usually done by pet-advocacy groups who call shelters and ask for euthanization figures), the incredible volume of pets being killed by humans is staggering.

As the second half of our Mexican seaside sojourn drifted by, Ann and I spent our days taking in the sights, swimming and wandering the quaint streets of Playa del Carmen. But by night, we became an efficient culinary machine, dolling out 20-plus cans of Alpo to the hungry canine and feline residents of the small beach town, the way McDonald's shovels up hamburgers to the huddled masses. As business grew, the menu evolved.

Not only did we offer the old stand-bys mentioned above, but Ann and I created an Alpo Soufflé, Creme D'Alpo, and Silver's favorite, Alpo à la Orange, which actually had tiny pieces of lime in it as a result of my fears about the dogs catching scurvy. (I figured the disease might run rampant near the ocean.) Of course, all these fabulous dishes were nothing more than plain old dog food slapped on a plate, but our customers didn't mind my queer, gourmet fantasies—they were just happy for an easy meal.

As Perro Café flourished, Ann began to question whether or not it was such a bright idea to feed Playa's strays after all. The animals, she pointed out, might become habituated to eating at the Blue Parrot's room No. 17. And once we left, what would they do for sustenance? Eat small tourists?

I felt a pang of guilt. She was right. Was it fair to lavish the dogs and cats of the village with Romanesque banquets, then take it all away in a blink of an eye? Carefully, I pared back the size of the servings, and the number of plates being offered each night, so that no one single animal could fill up at Perro Café, lest he forget how to scrounge out of a garbage can. I even chased off animals who were eating more than a specially allotted number of calories per day.

Our last day arrived.

With the exception of Silver, none of the dogs or cats of Playa del Carmen hung around our room as we humped our luggage over to the front desk. Indeed, we spotted several dogs down on the beach, relaxing near the dock, scratching fleas and sniffing the coastal wind. They seemed to be thinking little of food. I scratched Silver's ears, then climbed into an awaiting taxi. "Bye-bye, Silver," I said, leaning out the window and offering a weak smile.

Silver grinned and wagged his tail, aware that our partnership had come to an end, aware that the most successful dining establishment on the Yucatan coast, was now just a mere memory.

He watched the cab back out into the street and, as we pulled away from the Blue Parrot, he trotted off down the beach.

I don't know how many dogs inhabit the beaches of French Polynesia and how happy they are, but at least in one beach resort I know of—Playa del Carmen, Quintana Roo, Mexico—the resident dog (and cat) population lives a happy and healthy life. And, when the occasional oddball tourist comes to visit, they even score a few free meals.

I Dreamed of African Lions

(Tanzania, 1997)

"When the lions finished wandering around Nicholson's tent, they then went to a bunch of porters who were sleeping in the open. They stepped between, across, and over the sleeping men, and finally decided that none of the sleepers met their culinary demands."
—Peter Hathaway Capstick, *The African Adventurers*

It is often said that East Africa boasts some of the greatest game parks in the world. This, I assure you, is true. How can I be so certain? I've been a traveler all my life, journeyed to remote parts of the world, and dealt with some pretty offbeat challenges. And never in all my travels have I been as scared, awed and fascinated as I was by one single night in Serengeti National Park, at a remote camp that few other tourists seem to visit. The camp is called Lobo Camp, and while I can proudly boast of many nights shivering away on cold mountain faces, on filthy bus station floors, and next to broken-down automobiles, nothing was ever as difficult as one night at Lobo.

My scary night took place in January 1997, while I was on assignment in East Africa for several publishers. After three weeks of hard, grueling work (i.e., fun), my wife Ann—always in tow, in case things go wrong—and I decided to take a break and signed up for a seven-day safari, across portions of Tanzania's famed Northern Circuit.

The Northern Circuit is something of a misnomer. Although the circuit takes in many of Tanzania's most beautiful national parks, there are numerous highways and dirt roads one can travel. In short, there is no set circuit. And getting lost somewhere along the way seems to be part of the average non-set circuit trip. Land Rover breakdowns are an added bonus.

For most travelers, a trip around the Northern Circuit begins in Arusha, Moshi, Dar es Salaam or Nairobi, and takes in portions of Lake Manyara National Park, Serengeti National Park, Maswa Game Reserve, Tarangire National Park, Olduvai Gorge, the Ngorongoro Conservation Area, and, sometimes, the Masai Mara Game Reserve in Kenya. Many travelers begin or end their circuit with a climb of Kilimanjaro in Kilimanjaro National

Park, or Mount Meru in Arusha National Park.

Our particular non-set circuit was something of a "blue light special" through this list—a short circuit, if you please, with stops at Lake Manyara, Olduvai Gorge, the Ngorongoro Crater and the eastern Serengeti.

One late January morning, Ann and I shuffled into downtown Moshi to get started. When we got to the tour operator's office, we learned there was a small controversy involving our safari. There were five clients for this particular trip: Ann and I, and a family of three Parisians. The Parisians had, apparently, paid quite a bit of money back in France for their safari and did not want to share a vehicle with any Americans. (Nor Australians, most likely.) Thus, Ann and I were rewarded with our own vehicle, which we shared with a driver, Odiambo Mtwomo, and the safari cook, Sifuni Pellangyo.

Odiambo was a short, round man with small, strange-looking cup-shaped ears, which we guessed might've fallen victim to some tribal ritual, like being duct-taped around a couple of tennis balls. Sifuni was just as short, and just as round, but he had a winning smile and a knack for making people want to eat whatever it was he was cooking. "Call me Pellangyo," he said.

We loaded up two Land Rovers and hit the roughest highway in the universe out of Moshi, the Austral-American Land Rover following the French National Land Rover in a race for disaster (the Austral-American/French National Land Rover Disaster Race).

The great savannah of northern Tanzania rolled out before us like an infinite ocean of green and red hills. Dry plains of tall grass were punctuated by areas of thick scrub and dusty creek beds. Zebras, gazelles and secretary birds dotted the tawny expanses on the side of the road. Occasionally,

a Masai herdsman would appear on the horizon, and stand watching—grinning ear to ear—as we bounced by. Clearly, they mistook our efforts to keep our teeth seated in our gums as friendly smiles.

If there's one thing for which Africa sets the world standard, it would be crappy roads. Roads in Africa aren't only hard and rutted, they have a mysterious repetitive quality whereby the hardest protrusions are repeated at set intervals. Once you are mobile, these repetitive protrusions create a type of harmonic rhythm. At five miles per hour, the bumps feel like a rough sea, at 15 m.p.h. they feel like a ride on a wheat threshing machine and at 25 m.p.h. they make you feel as though you've been crammed inside a giant electric toothbrush that is subsequently switched on and thrown over a cliff. Unfortunately, you cannot speed out of this rhythm—beyond 25 miles per hour one literally risks bouncing off the road. A typical African journey by road is enough to make you physically and mentally ill.

The British response to the situation seems to have been the introduction of the Land Rover, a vehicle with a suspension system that is politely described as wooden, but perhaps more accurately described as broken. Land Rovers don't bounce over ruts, they explode over ruts. They don't cushion their occupants, they shatter them. Moreover, seats in a Land Rover are designed for metal boxes, not frail human musculature.

By midafternoon on our first day, it was painfully clear that this trip would not only be an assault on the tactile senses, it would also be an assault on the auditory facilities: Odiambo had only one cassette—of awfully bad reggae, if that's possible—to last an entire week.

Late in the afternoon of our first day, we arrived at Lake Manyara National Park for an evening game drive. Games drives are an interesting safari side-event. They are, in the most simple terms, drives through national parks to watch animals. They are held at sunrise and sunset when the animals are feeding, and their main purpose is to allow safari-goers a better chance to see the local wildlife than middle-of-the-day visits. At sunrise or sunset on any given day in hundreds of African parks, you can see thousands of tourists' heads poked merrily out the roofs, windows and doors of minivans, Land Rovers and other safari-type vehicles as they eagerly scan the horizon with binoculars and cameras for fauna.

If you've ever been to East Africa, you'll know that games drives are dependent primarily on a vehicle operator's ability to actually spot game, then drive as close as possible without frightening the beasts away. Really top-notch safari drivers have honed their skills over years of driving.

Our driver, Odiambo, was a bottom-notch driver. He missed dozens of interesting animals that Ann and I could easily see from miles away—things like elephants walking alongside the road. To make up for his embarrassingly well-developed inability to spot wildlife, he would speed toward clusters of other vehicles—obviously pulled up around a creature—before slapping on the brakes and coming to a shuddering stop among the crowd. This generally had the affect of producing a large brown cloud of dust that would then settle over everyone and everything, with the end result being that the animals we'd all come to enjoy would wander off coughing.

Odiambo's only obvious skill was sleeping in, which meant that by the time we got him his morning coffee and had pushed him into the Land Rover behind the wheel, it was generally far too late in the day for animal activity of any kind. It was much like going to look at the circus tent after the elephants and acrobats had left town. Still, we were stuck with Odiambo, and he was an okay guy, all in all.

Lake Manyara National Park is something of a study in contrasts. To reach the park gate, one drives through the village of Mto-Wa-Mbu (which translates as the inviting "Mosquito River") before crossing the park boundary into the national park itself. The bustling, colorful village, with its several thousand residents, is immediately supplanted by a quiet, pristine jungle filled with creatures of all kinds. There, the lake sits on some of the flattest plains in Tanzania yet butts up against the steep escarpment on the western side of the Great Rift Valley fault. It's a strange sort of topography.

We did two game drives through the park. Once in the evening and once the following morning (after a half hour spent waking Odiambo who clearly wasn't worried about missing anything), both times awed that such a vast array of wildlife could exist within spitting distance of a busy village.

We spent a night at the luxurious Twiga Campground, in Mto-Wa-Mbu, sipping cold beer and watching British filmmaker Alan Root's horrendously graphic videos about Africa's Big Five predators: the lion, the cheetah, the leopard, the wild dog and the hyena. As an impala was torn limb from limb by a pack of wild dogs on the flickering screen, I began to wonder about our plans for two nights of camping in the Serengeti. The African predators we were learning about on video looked utterly demonic. The video wound down, and seemed about to end.

"But there really are six predators!" the television suddenly blared. Ann and I thought the credits were next; instead, we were treated to some particularly graphic gore. "Because no story on predators would be complete if it didn't include THE CROCODILE!" (Dah-da-hah! More tearing flesh and spattering blood.)

The next day, we set out for the Ngorongoro Crater, the so-called Eighth Natural Wonder of the World. A journey there begins with a climb up out of the Great Rift Valley into the lush montane forests of the Ngorongoro Highlands. Majestic turacos flitted quickly over the roof of the Land Rover, and here and there dik-diks ran for cover in the thick forest. Ann and I gazed out our open roof most of the day, enjoying the breeze and the views. Around two p.m., suddenly and without warning, the road did a 90-degree turn and had it not been for Odiambo's NASCAR-like skills (and a big tree), we would have careened down 2,000 feet of steep mountainside into the crater below.

The Ngorongoro Crater is fantastic. One of the world's finest monuments to volcanic activity, the depression is some 15 kilometers wide and 600 meters deep. It is thought to be 2.5 million years old, and the volcano from which it originated is believed to have once been as tall as Kilimanjaro. The crater floor houses several permanent springs that bubble up to form Lake Magadi, a muddy, flat-bottomed marsh which attracts thousands of birds.

Most visitors to East Africa are well-versed in stories and statistics about the region's mammals (Alan Root videos get around), but East Africa also boasts some 1,293 documented bird species. Compared with the roughly 250 species found in Great Britain, and the roughly 850 species found in North America, East Africa's birds are a wonder unto themselves. As we pulled up next to Lake Magadi, ducks, geese, flamingoes, storks, cranes, vultures, kingfishers and several species of plover strolled about in the shallow water, casually poking here and there in search of food. As with birds, many species of East African animals can be found within the Ngorongoro Crater. We pulled up, showered the birds in a layer of dust and watched as they walked away coughing.

Not much later, we joined a long line of safari vehicles crossing the floor of the crater. About the same time, a half dozen rhinos decided to cross the crater floor perpendicular to the vehicular traffic. Since motor vehicles aren't allowed off the narrow road, the arrival of the rhinos caused quite a stir among safari drivers and they all spent 20 minutes jockeying for the best position along the narrow road. Of course, when the rhinos got a little closer, and it became apparent the best rhino-viewing might be another few hundred yards down the road, there was a manic reshuffling of automobiles (plumes of brown dust) as 25 over-eager safari drivers jockeyed for position. By the time everyone thought they were in place, the rhinos were long gone.

We camped that night at a place called Simba Camp, a spectacular place on the crater rim. Surrounded by lush forests filled with elephants, rhinos, buffaloes and numerous species of predator, Simba Camp is patrolled by park rangers carrying M-16s. Two of these friendly chaps—armed to the teeth with bandoleer upon bandoleer of huge cartridges—walked around the perimeter of the camp for the entire night, occasionally shining their flashlights into the dense forest surrounding camp. (I don't know exactly what they saw, but when I pointed my anemic flashlight out into the forest, a thousand glowing eyes of all size, elevation and proximity stared back. Clearly, I needed my own weapon.)

At two a.m., my bladder decided to make an appearance and I arose for a leak. I carefully unzipped our tiny mountaineering tent's nylon door, and stepped out, crouching, onto the wet grass. Of course, crouched next to a tent in the darkness wearing only a pair of briefs, I was either likely to (a) surprise the heck out of the soldiers, which would result in my being gunned to death, (b) surprise the heck out of a hyena, which would result in my being mauled to death, or (c) surprise the heck out of Ann, which would surprise the heck out of the soldiers, which would result in my being gunned to death.

It was a serious predicament, as any of the three might've resulted in my becoming a former person. If the hyenas didn't drag me off and crunch my limbs to powder, the local rangers might mistake me for some gangly white African yeti and shoot me. Option three—surprising Ann—would likely have yielded a similar result: a swift military action by the rangers. I made a nervous splattery mess all over myself next to the tent, and crawled back inside.

Our next stop was Olduvai Gorge, a dry, shallow unimpressive canyon, where human fossils dating back 3.7 million years were found by Mary and Louis Leakey toward the end of the last century. Exactly how the Leakeys knew to dig for anything in Olduvai Gorge is a total mystery to me. Let's look at the facts objectively: dry, horrible place with man-eating beasts, too many flies, a gift shop with runny ice cream, and thousands of miles from anywhere sensible. Hmm. Sounds like a place to avoid. I can totally understand early humans evolving in Southern China, where there's plenty of rainfall and lots of greenery, or perhaps a Mexican beach resort or maybe the South of France with its excellent wines, but if I were Australopithecus, I doubt Olduvai Gorge would've been a huge turn on for me. A web page I recently read about Olduvai Gorge noted, "when you actually stand there and imagine early hominids walking around this landscape, it can get pretty spooky and thrilling." Bloody hot and bloody boring, more like. Anyway, the Leakeys dug and they discovered, and today the canyon has become something of a cult shrine for amateur anthropologists and archaeologists much the same way the Pro-Wrestling Hall of Fame is a shrine for skinny 14-year olds.

Admittedly, by the time we reached Olduvai Gorge, Ann and I had become more attuned to the wildlife of Northern Tanzania and we spent most of our time at Olduvai Museum looking for animals (the most interesting being some brightly colored lizards). As the hot sun climbed to its zenith over our heads, we set off for what I considered the main event—the Serengeti.

Serengeti National Park, established in 1951, is Tanzania's oldest and biggest national park. Most would agree it is also Tanzania's grandest. Not only is the park home to millions of animals, its wide open plains, broad acacia trees, blue skies and lonely kopjes (pronounced "koppees," which are rocky hills) exemplify every human's concept of Africa. Yes, when you dream of Africa, you dream of the Serengeti.

My limited knowledge of the Serengeti came from a book called *My Serengeti Years* by Myles Turner. Turner was the warden of Serengeti National Park between 1956 and 1972, and was responsible for some of the most important wildlife conservation Africa has ever seen. Turner's early career was as a professional big game hunter in Kenya. Then, he landed the job of Serengeti warden, where he learned that the greatest threat to the wildlife of the Serengeti was poaching. A year after he took over the park, he initiated an historic campaign to rid the Serengeti of the thousands of poachers who preyed upon the park's creatures. As far back as 1957, it was estimated that 150,000 animals were poached annually.

Turner's methods were extremely effective, and he began capturing poachers in droves and confiscating their wire snares (the poachers' most popular tools). By 1971, the height of his anti-poaching war, Turner and his small group of dedicated rangers were arresting between 300 to 400 poachers annually and confiscating between 2,000 to 3,000 wire snares.

"The reader may well wonder how it is that any game has survived that unremitting carnage," Turner wrote. "There are three main reasons. First, sheer numbers alone have defied every effort at extermination. Secondly, every year for up to six months at a time, the great wildebeest and zebra herds are scattered far and wide across the central and eastern plains [of the

Serengeti], many miles from the nearest village. Thirdly, the presence of the tsetse fly has resisted any attempts at settlement and cultivation."

Although Turner died in 1984, he is probably resting very well indeed. Today the Serengeti's wildlife populations are as large as they have ever been, and international interest in the park has prompted Tanzanian government officials to maintain a high level of anti-poaching vigilance. If you ever get to camp in the Serengeti, you'll see the fruit of Turner's labors. On our first night there, at Seronera Camp, dozens of impalas, Thompsons gazelles, waterbucks, reedbucks, giraffes, buffaloes, and warthogs wandered brazenly through the camp. Never had I seen such a grand parade of fauna. Meanwhile, dozens of olive baboons scampered around the tents stealing bits and pieces of food, tubes of toothpaste, cameras and film, baseball caps, sunscreen, pocketknives and other accouterments that were really useful and hard to find in Africa.

Two nights camping at Seronera were punctuated by game drives. Each morning (latish, so Odiambo could sleep in) and evening, we'd drive five to ten miles along dirt roads criss-crossing the central portion of the park, watching the massive herds of ungulates and the powerful predators who followed them. Odiambo was oblivious, of course, but we knew this was classic Africa. Especially the grand vistas from the tops of small hills, where thousands of creatures could be seen in a single view.

Some repeat visitors to Tanzania claim the Serengeti has been ruined by tourism. I'd disagree. We saw every species of wild game we'd ever read about (from a cheetah mother with three kittens to a leopard hauling an impala carcass up a tree). The only real challenge, of course, was the out-of-control Game Drive Derby.

Regardless of the stock-car racing around camp, Seronera was wonderfully stimulating. There were some over-aggressive, thieving baboons; a surprise thunderstorm that flooded the camp, drained into our tent and soaked our belongings; and some manic Spaniards we met and socialized with (until they found out we lived in the United States and wanted to argue politics). Despite our enjoyment of the camp, our itinerary called for us to move on.

And this was how, on January 24, 1997, I ended up in Lobo Camp, the ultimate wild camp in the ultimate national park, and my ultimate camping experience. Pellangyo, the cook, had suggested we avoid Lobo Camp, the reputed second home of many seasonal poachers, but I was adamant. Lobo sounded wild!

The day began with a drive from Seronera to the north, along rough, rutted roads and over low hills. Ann and I stood for much of the drive with our heads out the roof as the animals were becoming more abundant. Topis, impalas, elephants and other creatures were commonplace, but we also saw less common creatures like jackals and elands.

As the day progressed, we also noticed that the farther we drove, the more lions we passed. In our first hour along the Lobo Camp road, we saw a group of three lions comprised of a mother and two cubs. Then, during our second hour of driving, we saw three groups of four lions. In our third hour, we saw about a half dozen groups of lions, six in each group. As we crept north, the number of lions kept growing, until, shortly before Lobo camp, we came across a group of eight lions (three mothers and five cubs) lying a few feet from the road. It was also clear that there were no other safaris around. We'd just spent four hours driving and had not once encountered another would be safari-NASCAR team.

Right about then I was starting to worry, but Odiambo and Pellangyo reassured us that camping in such country was safe … as long as we stayed in the tents all night.

"No problem," Odiambo said. "The animals prefer to eat each other." Not exactly the personalized, sympathetic reassurance I had been looking for. I suggested Odiambo become a counselor for prospective Serengeti park rangers. We arrived at Lobo Camp and set up tents and tables, and Pellangyo set to work building a feast.

Around dusk, as we huddled around a roaring fire eating a hot meal of soup and lamb, large hyenas began wandering through the middle of our little campsite. The first time I saw one of these creatures up close, I nearly fainted. Hyenas have three qualities that make them your worst nightmare: size, crushing power and boldness.

But what really struck me about hyenas was their size. Once night had descended over the Serengeti, and Ann and I were bundled in close to the fire with the three French and Odiambo and Pellangyo nearby, it was remarkable just how large these beasts are—we're talking about animals the size of small horses.

Through the blood-and-gore-filled Alan Root videos back in Mosquito River, I had learned that, indeed, the hyena belongs to its own family (*Hyaenidae*) and has the most powerful jaws of any land mammal and likely the most powerful jaws of any creature on earth in proportion to its size. With such powerful jaws, "a hyena can support its own weight by its jaws—it can actually hang by its jaws from a larger animal," according to "The Hyena Pages," on the web. They can chomp through "tusks, bone, hoofs, antlers and even teeth," not to mention, I'm sure, small safari vehicles driving away from Lobo Camp, airplanes leaving Tanzania and my bolted front door back in Colorado.

Not only that, these giant skull-crushing mammals—with their hunched gate and bloodshot stares—were penetrating well into camp. There's a sort of comfortable distance at which animals stay when one has a roaring blaze on the East African plain. These hyenas, however, didn't seem to recognize comfortable and casually strolled between us and the Land Rovers, us and the tents, us and each other. They pranced past as if testing our fear or, perhaps, waiting to be offered a camp chair. By the time dinner was over, several extremely large hyenas had casually tromped to within 20 feet of the protective fire, just to sniff around. Okay, we're told. This is normal for Lobo Camp. "No problem," Odiambo said. "The animals prefer to eat each other."

An hour later, we began the process of preparing for a night's sleep. The fire was out, and the hyenas that were everywhere an hour earlier had mysteriously disappeared. It appeared to me they had been scared off by some unusually deep roars that had been emanating from various points around the camp.

Ann and I were given one tent to sleep in, and the French contingent were given two tents. Odiambo said he would sleep in the truck. Pellangyo said he'd also sleep in the truck. I inquired, but was told there was only room for two small Africans in the vehicles, not two Africans and a gangly white man. "No problem," I thought to myself. "The animals prefer to eat each other."

Ann fell asleep as soon as her head hit the ground. Then, as if on cue, she began snoring. Now I don't have a problem with Ann snoring at home—she's welcome to cut up all the logs she wants—but here, at Lobo

Camp, surrounded by as-of-yet-to-be-identified creatures making similarly deep nasal grunts, I feared that they might mistake Ann's respiratory symphony as some kind of primordial greeting and want to get inside the tent.

This is what is so startling about camping in Africa. As soon as night falls, a bizarre cacophony of roaring sounds begins to emanate from every dark corner around the typical camp. I went to the zoo once as a kid, and hundreds of times as an adult, but none of the sounds I ever heard at the zoo matched the real thing on the Serengeti plain.

As I lay wide-eyed next to my partner, the snoring, the roaring, and some really desperate screeching noises continued unabated throughout the night. At approximately two a.m., while I was shivering in fear, I heard footsteps crushing the grass around the exterior wall of the tent—a sort of sssh-sssh-sssh sound, as large feet crushed the tall, dry blades and stalks. The footsteps went down one side of the tent, past my feet, then came up the other. Just as I reached out and clasped a hand over Ann's nose and told her to shush, something big scraped against the corner of the tent near my head.

Ann looked up from her slumber and lowered her brow.

"What are you doing?" she whispered.

"Sssh," I said again, certain that a set of ferocious teeth and angry claws were about to rip down the side of the tent and haul me screaming into the darkness. The soft-but-heavy footsteps circumnavigated the tent once more, and then stopped as if trying to decide whether this green, canvas box was worthy of an attack.

I huddled in silence.

Lions scare me but they fascinate me too. We all known the story of Tsavo, where the building of a railroad across Kenya by the British was halted by two man-eating tigers who devoured some 135 men (according to *The New York Times*, June 20, 1947) before being dispatched by Col. John Patterson.

Man has long had a sturdy sense of respect for the great cats, and with good reason. Lions can rip through cloth, boards and sheet metal if they really want to get at lunch. (At least that's what they showed in the film *The Ghost & The Darkness*, which depicted the events at Tsavo.) Such respect has made the creature the symbol of hundreds of world leaders and nations, including England.

In Greek mythology, Cybele, the mother goddess of Phrygia, rides a chariot drawn by lions. Heracles (Hercules) is regularly pictured wearing the skin of a lion. In Roman mythology, lions drew the chariot of Juno. In Hinduism, the fourth avatar of Vishnu is a lion. In Buddhism, the lion is Defender of the Law, and often statues of Buddha (who was called the Lion of the Shakya) are seated on a lion throne. In every Asian and African nation—and most European countries as well—the lion holds a lofty place in the psyche.

When you see them lying spread-eagled on their backs in the sun, next to the most popular watering holes in Africa, and without a care in the world except perhaps major protein digestion, you realize just how true the term King of the Jungle really is. There are few other creatures so well-respected by all the other animals. Hyenas, leopards, cheetahs, wild dogs and crocodiles might be feared by your typical Thompsons gazelle, but only a few of these creatures breed fear in the hearts of everyone. And certainly not all the time. Lions do both.

Historically, lions lived throughout much of Africa, Asia and southeastern Europe (including most of Greece and Macedonia). Centuries ago, there were a dozen different species of the great cat, including the Angola lion, the Asiatic lion, the Barbary lion, the Cape lion, the Masai lion, the Senegalese lion, and the Transvaal or South African lion.

The Barbary was possibly the lion with the best-remembered impact on man. This was the lion that once inhabited huge swaths of North Africa, and was the animal to which Romans fed Christians.

"In recent historic times the range of the Barbary lion was from Tripoli through Tunisia, Algeria, and Morocco," wrote David May in *Vanished Species*. "The last lion in the Pashalik of Tripoli was killed in 1700. The

last Tunisian lion was killed in 1891 ... and the last Algerian lion was killed the same year."

The Cape lion didn't even last as long as the Barbary. One of several subspecies in South Africa, with an unknown range, it was common across the Cape Province and around Capetown. Of course, the concerns of settlers prompted an eradication effort, and in 1858 the last Cape lion known in Cape Province was killed. The last known creature of the species was killed by a General Bisset in Natal, in 1865.

"A couple of years ago, Dr. Hym Ebedes of the Onderstepoort Veterinary Institute in South Africa was checking out a zoo in Addis Ababa, Ethiopia when he stumbled across eleven lions that fit the description of either the Cape or the Barbary lions," wrote lion enthusiast Steve Warmack on his Hodge-Podge website. "They had the huge manes and the heavy bodies of either species. It turns out that the cats are descendants of a group kept by Emperor Haile Selassie at the royal palace in Addis before his regime was toppled by a 1974 coup. Selassie called his dynasty the Lions of Ethiopia and kept them around as symbols of power. With his overthrow, the zoo got the lions." Exactly what species of lion they were has never been determined.

Although the lion is still considered vermin in some parts of Africa prompting it to be shot as a pest, there are an estimated 30,000 to 40,000 in Africa, and another estimated 200 to 360 in the Gir Forest of Northwestern India.

Meanwhile, back at Lobo Camp, I was nearing dismemberment. The lion prowling around the tent had stopped and was undoubtedly ready to pounce, tear, and devour. If that wasn't bad enough, I had smashed my hand over my wife's snoring face with a little more force than was necessary and she was now glaring at me with incredibly pissed-off eyes. I thought she might, as the saying goes, throw me to the lions.

Fortunately, at that very

moment, Michel, the elder Frenchman in the tent next to ours, began snoring very loudly. Very, very loudly. The grass-crushing creature, whatever it was, strode off to investigate.

What is wrong with the French? Do they have underdeveloped sinuses? Michel motored along like the Orient Express. I lay wide awake in my sleeping bag for the remainder of the night, listening to Michel and thinking of large factories with bad plumbing. The matter of the lion vanished from thought and all I could think about was sinus spray commercials. ("Sinus pressure keeping you from your best day at work? Try Evacu-Head … ")

Ann, of course, hadn't been the least bit bothered by the huge creatures wandering through our camp, grunting, snorting and growling like professional wrestlers. Or Michel's breathing. She went straight back to sleep and her own version of bad plumbing.

In the morning, I found out a lot that I probably didn't want to know the night before. According to Pellangyo, who had been watching out the front of the truck, our camp had been visited by at least a half dozen lions during the night. The creature that had grazed the side of the tent—just a few inches from my head—was, yes indeed, a large male lion, out for a night of hunting, fighting, carousing and doing whatever lions do at night. This lion had, in fact, made two trips around our tent before wandering off to investigate the Frenchman's snoring. Luckily for me, my head was still upon my shoulders and I retained all four limbs. Perhaps the only things shredded to the point of no return were my nerves. I wandered over to the small fire that Pellangyo had started and made myself a cup of coffee. Odiambo stood next to the flickering flames, sipping from a similar cup.

"How was your night?" Odiambo asked, smiling.

"No problem," I said, smiling back. "The animals prefer to eat each other."

The remainder of our safari was pretty tame. We drove north and east through the Grumeti River Valley to Lake Natron, where some 200,000 flamingoes live, then back to Lake Manyara. Everything went pretty much as planned, except for a minor breakdown in three-foot-deep dust, which was fixed within half an hour. (Apparently Land Rovers don't like excessive dust.)

We ended up back in Moshi and sacked out in our hotel room. Later, as the evening sun descended over the western horizon, and Kilimanjaro went from soft blue to hazy purple, Ann and I cleaned ourselves up and went out into the hotel courtyard to socialize. A pair of young Australians were drinking beer and flipping through a guidebook. We immediately struck up a conversation about safariing, and the great game parks of Northern Tanzania.

After a few minutes, one of the two became deadly serious, and leaned across the table. "My biggest concern is the wildlife," he said with a furrowed brow. "I'm really scared of animals. Are they dangerous?"

I smiled, took a long sip of Coke, winked at Ann, and answered, "No problem. The animals prefer to eat each other."

The Arachnids of Arenal

(Costa Rica, 1994)

"Take time to watch the bugs!"
—Harry S. Pariser, *The Adventure Travel Guide to Costa Rica*

As I lay sleepily on the bed of our Manuel Antonio bungalow, watching the Costa Rican forest sway gently outside the open door, a blood-curdling scream echoed from the closet.

It wasn't the normal kind of cry my wife normally made in times of distress—a fairly simple girlish shriek or something along those lines. No, this was something much more frightening, a deep, deranged howling kind of moan, one that grew in volume and tone until it crescendoed as an unnerving dog-with-tail-slammed-in-car-door-like wail. I pulled my heart out of my throat and leapt from the bed. Had she found a body? Had a trap door opened in the wardrobe floor revealing a pit of deadly vipers? Had she sliced off her legs, arms and teeth while shaving?

The answer came almost instantly. Ann ran towards the open door and flung a dark blue cotton T-shirt outside. It hit the ground limply. Then, I watched in astonishment as something moved within the folds. It was a thin, sticklike creature. The creature disentangled itself from the folds of cotton and crawled onto the nearby concrete footpath. Once on solid ground, it flattened itself. Then it started running down the path. It was a scorpion, and one of the proudest specimens I'd ever seen. Some eight inches in length (when it flattened out to run) it was a light translucent brown, with bluish-black claws and pincers.

Ann's scream hadn't gone unnoticed. On the walkway outside our room, a small crowd of gardeners, hotel maids and fellow tourists had quickly gathered. One of the gardeners, a fellow named Jose (Jose Number One, for this story), spotted the fleeing scorpion and promptly stepped on it, smashing the poor creature's body into a creamy pulp. He squatted down and studied it for several minutes as the crowd dispersed. Then, he looked up at me: "Muy Peligrosso!"

He shook his head several times to indicate that Ann had narrowly escaped with her life. With the index finger of his left hand curled like an eagle talon, he looked me in the eye, and stabbed at the palm of his other hand: "ESSTINGA!!!"

Jose Number One stood up and using his boot wiped the remainder of the pulpy scorpion body from the sidewalk and into the garden. With that, he turned and walked away. It took me several minutes to find someone who could speak English, and after a trial-by-fire sort of interrogation, I learned that not only was my Spanish still terrible, but that this particular model of scorpion was not found locally. It was from the central highlands of Costa Rica, the mountainous region that makes up the spine of this small Central American nation. After much gesticulating and back-and-forth translation, we all agreed that this fellow's particular trip to Manuel Antonio from the mountains had likely been in our luggage. And, this particular type of scorpion, Jose Number One assured me, was deadly.

Ann and I had planned our trip to Costa Rica in the summer of 1994. It was to be our honeymoon, and rather than travel with a tour group, we had opted to fly to San Jose then pick out whatever mini-adventures appealed to us on a day-by-day basis.

Size is, perhaps, Costa Rica's greatest appeal. The quaint Central American nation is so small—just 200 miles from the Nicaraguan border to the north and Panama to the south—that it's possible to drive across the entire nation in an afternoon.

In 1949, this forward-thinking country did away with its army and invested a healthy chunk of the savings into education and social services. Indeed, education officials from Europe are regularly sent to Central America to study the Costa Rican system. The literacy rate is regularly in the mid-90s, percentage-wise.

But it's perhaps the area of nature where Costa Rica shines brightest. More than one-quarter of the entire country has been set aside and preserved in its natural state, in the form of national parks or preserves. Its wildlands are a botanical wonderland of flora and fauna and scared tourists. Costa Rica boasts an estimated 9,000 species of plants, 1,200 varieties of orchids, 800 species of ferns, 850 species of birds, ten percent of all the world's butterflies, and 5,000 different species of grasshoppers. Intriguingly, over half the known mammal species in the nation—200 altogether—are bats. (There are an estimated 103 species of bats, with more likely to be found.)

So, my new bride and I went. We knew we'd see some birds; we hoped to see a few mammals. We were eager to visit the national parks, and partake in some adventure activities. We had little idea all of our adventures would be shared by Costa Rica's vast population of arachnae.

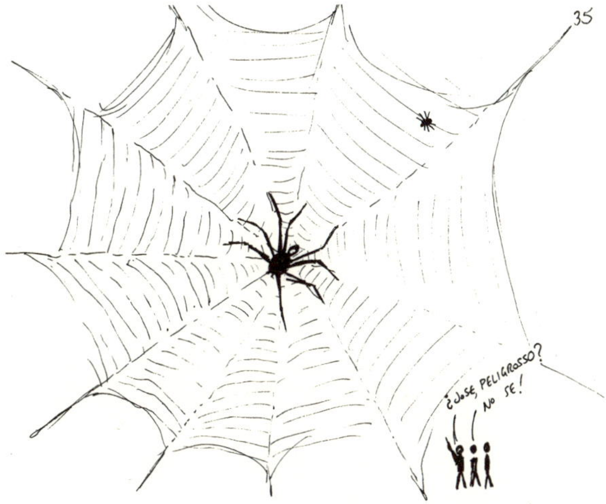

Our first jaunt was a three-day stint touring Tortuguero National Park. We were loaded into a tour bus and were shuttled through Braulio Carillo National Park. Our tour guide, Alberto, pointed out the spectacular waterfalls and canyons, the lush forest and the exotic birds. Halfway through the park, Alberto produced a jar from inside his backpack. It contained a bright yellow, highly venomous eyelash viper. The driver pulled over, and Alberto, in showmanship fashion, released the creature into the grass at the edge of the road.

"This little fellow was in the courtyard behind my apartment," he explained. "I wanted to make sure he returned to the forest. They are extremely dangerous, so stand back please."

Next stop was a banana processing facility, along the road to Limon. Here, Alberto pulled out a bunch of green bananas, then immediately dropped the bunch to the ground. An enormous green tarantula crawled out from the bunch and reared up, ready to strike. "Very dangerous," he said.

We moved on to Tortuguero, where we toured the fabulous canals and observed sloths in Tortuguero's trees. Our visit concluded with a hike up Cerro Tortuguero, an 800-foot hill offering views into neighboring Nicaragua. Spider webs were everywhere. Near the top of Cerro Tortuguero, we came across an especially intricate mosaic of webs adorning the bushes and trees on one side of the trail. Our guide, Jose (Jose Number Two), studied the intricate designs, and pointed out the tiny, delicate creatures sitting at the epicenter of each web. Ann and I collectively shivered. There were so many webs in such a small area, I couldn't count them all. It was like a collection of transparent kites, all piled one on top of another.

"Peligrosso?" I asked pointing at the maze of webs.

"No se."

"It looks pretty peligrosso, dontcha think?"

"Que?" Jose Number Two shrugged and wandered off down the trail. Ann and I ran after him.

Our next adventure took us down the Pacuare River on a rubber raft. We spent two days bouncing down rapids and through eddies, stopping occasionally for a meal, or a side trip to examine flora, fauna and geologic wonders. We spent our only night on the trip in a rustic jungle bungalow, the kind of place that was crawling with insect life. Before going to sleep we spent a few minutes sweeping the nooks and crannies of the wooden hut free of critters, especially the few that looked like they might make a break for our bed in the night.

In the morning as we loaded the boats, there was another evil-sounding shriek. This time it was a Dutch woman, a fellow tourist. She had spotted one of the biggest spiders any of us had ever seen. She screamed and ran back up on the beach. The rest of us stood ankle deep in the river and wondered if Costa Rica had piranhas.

The spider, we were informed when our guide Manuel caught it, was a Jesus Christ spider. With a body the size of a quarter and eight long legs that gave the animal a seven-inch span, this particular spider had the remarkable ability to run across water. He was fast, too, capable of maintaining a flat-out gallop for hundreds of feet at a time. Jesus Christ was a good name; Sea Biscuit might've been more appropriate.

Anyway, this impressive arachnid had presumably been hunting something or other on the river's surface (my guess is small whales), then frightened by our arrival on the beach, had taken refuge in one of the boats. Manuel checked the rafts inside and out and declared them free of spiders and fit for "continued whitewater action."

I don't know how ready the rest of the group was for continued whitewater action, but we carefully climbed into the rafts and checked them thoroughly.

According to entomologists, spiders are found all over the world in vast quantities. Supposedly, over a million of them can be found in an average one-acre grassy field and they've been found as high as 23,000 feet in the Himalayas. There are about 2,500 different species in North America, and an estimated 34,000 species worldwide. No one knows exactly how many species of spider Costa Rica has, but by the time we were settled back inside the yellow raft on the Pacuare River, we were guessing that the natural distribution process had favored Central America.

Indeed, the few difficult-to-find tidbits I'd read about Costa Rican spiders are frightening, especially the information about the tarantulas. Costa Rica is famous for its tarantulas. There are green tarantulas, orange-kneed tarantulas, red tarantulas, Costa Rican tigerrumps, pink-footed tarantulas, zebra tarantulas, curlyhair tarantulas—you name it. Some are reputed to build webs strong enough to snare hummingbirds. One folktale even holds that the silk from some tarantulas is so strong the indigenous people used it for fishing before filament was available. (The folktale explains nothing about the challenges of casting with a tarantula in your hand, but folktales never do.)

"I collected spiders," wrote poet Jonathan Teets after a visit to Costa Rica. "They lasted longer if covered with hairspray, though not long enough. Their legs would start to curl inward first. San Jose's tropical afternoon rains bring spiders out. Yellows, reds, purples. There were multicolored oxcarts in all the tourist traps, none so colorful as a single spider. It seemed there was only one of each species."

A few days later we headed for Arenal, a sleepy village in the Central Highlands surrounded by farms and coffee plantations. We rode the bus from San Jose (patron saint of all the Joses in Costa Rica, hence their natural prolific distribution in Central America) to Tilaran, thence by taxi cab to Arenal. Our goal on this particular mini-adventure had been Volcano Arenal but after a three-hour strangulation of the Spanish language, courtesy of yours truly, we wound up at a motel on the northwest edge of Lake Arenal, miles from the famed mountain, at around three a.m.

We were shown to rooms that were alive with insect life. Hundreds of cockroaches scurried back and forth across the floor. Moths buzzed around the lights like kamikaze pilots. Creatures of all shape, size, body configuration and leg count scurried across the bed. Ann, who's not a great fan of insects, held it together pretty well until she ventured into the shower. There she was met by a gar-

gantuan cockroach (whom we later named King Roach) sitting near the water tap.

The encounter sent her recoiling towards me with a demand of getting her out of there. She clearly wasn't happy and standing over me, expressed this in several terse, Germanic-sounding words. As a giant hairy moth flew into her eye and got stuck there, she announced she was ready to have my head. I told her that was somewhat ironic since the females of many species of spiders eat their mates soon after copulation is complete. "In fact," I said cheerily, "with some species, the female mates, eats the male, then carries the babies around on her back until she dies. Then the babies eat her."

"Argh!" Ann said, just as a moth flew into her other eye.

We spent the night huddled together in a single cot, waving rolled-up magazines at the various flying predators, occasionally hitting one, occasionally being attacked and bitten … or stung, or whatever it was they were doing. I could hear King Roach chuckling to himself as he ran a hot bath.

The next morning we caught a bus to La Fortuna, the village we'd really meant to visit, which sits below the famous volcano. I found us a room at a tiny downtown hostel (only a few spiders under the bed, but some weird looking beetles on the window), and we wandered through the village taking in the sights. We enjoyed a festive lunch at the town's best restaurant, and that night visited the volcano and swam in some hot springs near its base.

The following day, after inquiring about the next bus out of town, Ann and I found ourselves with a full day to kill. So, at the advice of some locals, we signed up for a three-hour tour of the Cavernas de Venado. (For you non-Spanish speakers, that would be Venado Caves in English.)

Our guide to the caves, named (what else?) Jose showed us the entrance: a narrow limestone hole in a small rocky wall, with a fast stream issuing from the portal. To our astonishment, the rock walls around the mouth of the cave were covered with spiders. Not only the large Jesus Christ spiders, of which we'd become so fond of during our rafting adventure, but also other species no one seemed to know anything about.

"Peligrosso?" I asked pointing at the spiders.

"No se," Jose said.

"It looks pretty peligrosso, dontcha think?"

"Que?" Jose Number Three shrugged and ran into the cave.

Ann and I studied the mouth of the cave. Jose Tres, who was 40 feet inside and looking back out at us, winked and waved for us to follow: "No problemo. Vamos."

I ran next, and Ann, reluctantly, came third. Inside, our cheap plastic flashlights illuminated the walls of the cave. The spiders, it seemed, were only congregated around the entrance. Inside, our only problem was bats, which were everywhere. One flew into my mouth. We roamed through the caves, from chamber to chamber, and examined the fantastic stalactites and stalagmites which dominated the bigger rooms. After what felt like several weeks we ran back out the entrance, happy to be alive. We took a taxi back to Fortuna and cleaned up for the bus ride back to San Jose, where we loaded up our belongings and caught a bus to the Pacific coast and Manuel Antonio National Park.

And this is when we really got to know Costa Rica's arachnids. Somehow during the next few days—as we journeyed from La Fortuna to San Jose to Manuel Antonio—our friend the eight-inch scorpion came with us. Whether he thought he was hiding in a safe spot, or whether

he was some rare, migratory species of backpack-dwelling scorpion, we'll never know. All Ann knows is that when we arrived in Manuel Antonio, she hung her wet t-shirt up, inside-out, in the closet. In the morning, she took the garment from its resting-place and began to turn it right-side out. That's when she discovered her hitchhiker and that evil wail began.

Of course, had her shirt been right-side out to begin with, she would have put it on straightaway. She'd never have flipped it right-side out and discovered the scorpion waiting inside. I shudder to think of the noise she might have made then. Once we'd both calmed down, we spent the morning going through every scrap of clothing we'd brought to Central America—dumping it on the floor, jumping on it repeatedly, smashing it with our fists, and ultimately throwing it all into the shower for a thorough rinsing. After much crumpling, we packed our bags and flew to San Juan, and made our way to the Hotel Don Carlos. Our new Anti-Scorpion Packing Process was repeated in the bathroom. Clothes were stomped on, screwed into tight balls, then flung into the shower where they were rinsed thoroughly.

We flew home the next day. My new bride told me that next time we planned a trip to the tropics, it would be to sit on a warm beach and sleep in a clean hotel; no jungle adventures, no spider-riddled caves, no King Roach motels. In other words, none of my adventurous crap. Of course, Ann and I are still married, and occasionally she reminds me of our creepy-crawly honeymoon.

The United States boasts some 40 different species of scorpionida arachnida, only one of which is deadly. There are some 1,400 species worldwide, many of which can produce a neurotoxin which destroys the nervous system, ultimately causing death. Whatever species our hitchhiking friend was, no one in Manuel Antonio seemed to know and we'll likely never find out.

We like to think of him as our adventure guide, so we called him—what else?—Jose.

Bathtubs Along the Ewaso Ngiro

(Kenya, 1997)

"Rationalization afforded us little comfort."
—David Brower, *For Earth's Sake*

The Ewaso Ngiro is a small, crooked river that runs east-west across the thorny scrub country of north central Kenya, halfway between Lake Turkana and Mt. Kenya. For much of its length, the Ewaso Ngiro traverses an area known as the Samburu Tribal District, named in honor of the friendly, colorful Samburu tribe, which lives and prospers under the boiling equatorial sun.

A decade or so ago, an enterprising British expatriate named Malcolm Gasciogne bought a few acres of rolling bush country on the outskirts of a Samburu village called Marallal. There, he constructed a rustic hotel and a restaurant, hired a few Samburu guides, and began running camel safaris across the dusty red plains, roughly following the Ewaso Ngiro. Adventure travelers the world over have visited Marallal for one or other of Gasciogne's safaris, and have left Kenya with fond memories of perhaps their most authentic African adventure.

In late February 1997, my old college climbing partner Benny Bach and I had just come down from Mt. Kenya after a month of hiking and climbing. We were wandering around Nairobi looking for something to fill the week before our departure back to the U.S. We were tired after a month on the mountain, and longed for something relaxing. The beach, perhaps? A tour of some of the game parks, maybe? A street hawker walked by and handed Benny a brochure, from a company called Yare Safaris.

"The Ultimate Adventure Safari" said the brochure. "Comfortable and well-attended camel safaris run on a weekly basis. Satisfaction guaranteed."

The brochure said we would travel 15 to 18 kilometers a day on camel back, along the banks of the Ewaso Ngiro (Brown River), guided by a Samburu *moran* (warrior), taking in the bountiful wildlife that dwells along the river's flanks. At the end of each day's ride, we were to be met by a support vehicle, loaded down with all the comforts of home.

"We do not recommend swimming in the Ewaso Ngiro as there are crocodiles," the brochure warned.

Camping out! Camel riding! Wild animals! Samburu Warriors! We raced over to Yare's Nairobi office and plonked down $400 apiece.

On Saturday, March 1, we were met by a minibus outside our Nairobi hotel. We climbed in and were seated behind two teenage English girls, Jenny and Sally, and a middle-aged Scottish woman named Moira. A chummy eight hours worth of bumpy roads later, we were in Marallal and we were all best friends. Marallal. Hmm … I suddenly realized this town sounded uncannily like malarial, and I had to wonder if we'd brought enough mosquito netting and repellent.

Despite its off-putting name, Marallal is a wonderful little town, where the streets are dirt, and the quaint wooden buildings with their rickety clapboard porches bring to mind the dusty towns of Hollywood westerns. Besides being quaint, Marallal is a Samburu town, and the Samburu is one of the friendliest tribes in Africa. When the Masai migrated to southern Kenya from the Sudan during the late Middle Ages, the Samburu splintered off, and decided to stay put in north central Kenya. The two tribes still speak the same language, and the word Samburu is derived from the Masai expression *ilsampurrum pur*, which means butterflies. Throughout the early European colonization of East Africa, the Samburu people were simply known as the Northern Masai, but after a series of Masai civil wars in the 1870s and 1880s, the Samburu assumed their own identity. The Samburu dress, culture and tribal practices are almost the same as those of their southern cousins. They drink warm goat's blood, circumcise young adults, and wear thousands of colorful beads and calf-length red robes.

We were unloaded at Yare Safari's small hotel on the outskirts of town. Yare, we quickly learned, is one of the most important businesses in town, and employs dozens of local Samburus who have become adept at helping Malcolm separate tourists from their hard-won cash. Despite its famous safaris, Yare's biggest claim to fame is the once-annual Marallal International Camel Derby, in which riders compete in three categories (professional, semi-professional and amateur) for over $10,000 in prize

money. So far the winners of the professional category have all been local Samburu safari guides, who have a close relationship with the resident camel population. Unfortunately, Benny and I were six months from the camel races, which are held in October, so we had to be content with a regular old safari.

That night, we were treated to a campfire and dinner out the back of the hotel, a sort of pre-celebration for the next six days. What we were pre-celebrating I'm not quite sure, but it was pleasant enough. We dined on roasted goat, rice and vegetables. I went back for seconds and thirds. One of the cooks, a wily gal named Connie, noted my dining superiority and called me *ngruwe* (Pig in Swahili). I liked this, and suggested it be modified to Bwana Ngruwe, or Mr. Pig. Benny liked this also and asked what the term was for hyena.

"*Fisi*," Connie said.

"Feces?" Benny and I asked in astonished unison.

"Fisi!" Connie said loudly, directing fast spittle at our faces. "Fisi, fisi, fisi."

As is so often the pattern whenever Benny and I are in an exotic land, we were soon off on a really weird tangent ("Stand back, Connie's about to blow!" "Are fisis endangered here?") and were both howling with laughter within just a few minutes. The hyena-like sound emanating from Benny earned him the nickname Bwana Fisi (Mr. Hyena), a name that would take

on considerable significance as our safari progressed.

During dinner, a tall, extremely thin Samburu warrior—holding a six-foot-long steel spear—walked over to join our gathering. His name, we were told, was Idi, and he was to be our guide. Idi, who wore a ankle-length pink dress, a few strands of beads and a huge *panga* (machete) strapped to his waist, looked strikingly like Sammy Davis, Jr. He was the only Samburu we would ever meet who didn't have gaping holes pierced through his ear lobes. I wondered if he knew the words to "That Old Black Magic."

We also met our safari supervisor, the fellow who was to drive the support vehicle, and meet us at our pre-arranged camps along the river. His name was Anthony, and he was a Kikuyu (like three million of Kenya's 30 million residents). Anthony was extremely eager to please, and spent the better part of the night explaining how this was his first safari as supervisor, and that things had to go smoothly, so that his boss—a white Briton—would trust him. As a young Kikuyu trying to make his way in an economically-depressed nation, a successful safari meant everything.

"Please! Please! Please!" Anthony told us every hour or so that night, "Anything you want, any problem you have, anything you don't like, please, please, please, just come to me."

The relationship between the blacks and whites in Kenya had made an impression in the three months I'd spent in East Africa. The local Africans try mightily to win respect and honor while many of the local whites treat the Africans pretty poorly. Once on Mt. Kenya, I saw a white tour group leader so incensed at his African Man Friday (screaming, throwing things, all those adult forms of communication) I thought a murder would soon follow.

The next day, after loading into a huge, purple ex-Army truck that had been customized with several bench seats for the safari business (not to mention Land Rover-style suspension), we were driven several hours in what appeared to be an easterly direction, towards the Ewaso Ngiro. About halfway there, we got a flat tire. We disembarked from the truck, waited patiently while the tire was changed, then resumed the drive. "So sorry!" Anthony said repeatedly. Another hour of rocky dirt road brought us to a cluster of green trees on a slope, near which were a collection of tents, tables, and two safari cooks working on a meal. A hundred feet down the slope was a curious expanse of sand and gravel.

"Here we are!" Anthony said merrily as he jumped out the door of the truck, "Camp One."

We peered out the truck window. "Where's the river?" I asked, stepping down from the vehicle. "You know, the Ewaso Ngiro? The Brown River."

"Down there, Bwana Ngruwe," Anthony said motioning toward the expanse, "It's a bit dry right now."

A bit dry was like saying lions have a few teeth. The Ewaso Ngiro was no more than a parched, flat expanse in a thorny, barren landscape. Death Valley is more lush. The three British women, Benny and I wandered down to the sandy, gravely riverbed and gazed at it in wonder. We looked "upstream," then "downstream." There were no pools of water, no puddles, not so much as a mud bog along the half mile or so we could see in either direction. There were no crocodiles, no gazelles, no elephants, no lions or hyenas. Just a few local children with herds of goats.

Certainly, the word *safari* doesn't have anything to do with wildlife. It means travel in Swahili, the language invented by Arab, Indian, and British colonizers of East Africa. Historically, however, most safaris have centered entirely around the activity of either game hunting, or game watching. Our Yare Camel Safari was going to focus—I surmised—on a strict translation of safari: to travel. Certainly, if lack of water in the Ewaso Ngiro hadn't driven the animals away, the 120-degree heat probably had. I swatted at the flies and, with the rest of the group, pondered the "nature" of our safari. When we arrived back at the tents, Anthony was backing the truck into a tree and spinning the wheels so furiously that a cloud of burnt rubber engulfed the scene. "I'll be back in a couple of hours," he said out the cab window. "I'm going to get the spare fixed."

Once Anthony had departed in a swirl of dust, Idi and two young Samburu morans, who had been hired to help Idi wrangle camels, introduced us to the five beasts we would be riding. My camel was named Jet. Strangely, Jet was the smallest of the bunch, despite the fact that I was easily the biggest tourist among the group. I stroked Jet's flank and said, "Hello, boy."

Jet immediately looked around to face whatever it was scratching his side and, with that warm, pleasant facial expression camels are known for, made a horrific noise, a cross between a donkey's neigh and sheet metal being dragged across a parking lot. His breath was the most wretched thing I have, in 36 years on this planet, ever breathed. With that as an appetizer, we retired to the camp for dinner.

Fortunately, Benny and I had had the presence of mind to pack two crates of beer in the truck before our departure from Marallal, and we immediately set to work emptying the crates. We handed out cold Tuskers—the most popular brand of local beer—to our cooks, our fellow safari clients, and to Idi, who despite his rail thin build could put away beer like an Olympic athlete.

As the orange sun slipped down over the western plains, we built a bonfire and talked about England, Scotland and America, and our collective adventures in East Africa—of travels we'd made, travels yet to make. As talk of this or that activity unfolded, we began to realize that our three British companions were all pretty snooty, and they tried to out-snoot each other with tales of powerful social events and high-reaching personal contacts they had back on the Mother Isle. There was a lot of interesting talk between Jenny and Sally regarding marriage to a lord, or a baron or someone with a family position. Moira, who seemed to be the most snobby of the three, assured the young girls they couldn't possibly marry into the particular families being mentioned. The whole scene was like something out of a bad 19th century romance novel.

Benny and I couldn't have cared less. We were trying to keep tabs on Idi, who was working his way through the crate of beer the way a Nairobi taxi driver weaves his way through pedestrians.

Day Three dawned same as all the rest—hot. Really hot. Unbelievably hot. Since our support truck was still missing—God knows what had happened to Anthony—

and we couldn't move camp, Idi decided we should just do a camel day-ride, a sort of abbreviated jaunt around the camp area, until Anthony returned with the truck.

The two young morans, whose names were Matthew and something that sounded like *Mbundo*, saddled up the camels and informed us they were ready to ride. The saddles were simple affairs—four pieces of wood encircling the camel's hump, and crudely lashed together with a short piece of hemp rope. A pillow was placed atop each "saddle" and the whole stinking, gangly assemblage was good to go.

And so we went: three skinny black men dressed in cool cotton robes and who'd grown up on camels followed by five extremely pasty white, soft-skinned, overfed, non camel riders. Whoever came up with the term *camel jockey* as a derogatory label for Arabic peoples needs to get his head examined. Anyone who can get on one of these beasts and successfully stay on for any period of time deserves all the respect in the world. As we bumped across the dry, gulch-like tributaries of the Ewaso Ngiro, I wished I were more Arab and less pasty white.

Our camels were the single-hump common dromedary camels, a species found across Arabia, North Africa and Australia. According to the experts, today there are no wild dromedaries left. All of them have reportedly been domesticated.

"The capacity of the dromedary to endure extremely long periods without water through a variety of physiological mechanisms, is unrivaled," states *Simon & Schuster's Guide to Mammals*. "Thus, it has become one of the most valuable transports for the inhabitants of the desert. It is easily domesticated, and can carry heavy loads."

As I thrashed up the hill on Jet, I wondered what the typical camel domestication process was. A lobotomy? A thorough beating? Idi sat sideways on his camel, looking back at us *mzungus* (Swahili for white person), and smiling broadly as we lurched and rumbled through the bush, our hair, eyes and clothes catching on the acacia tree thorns.

"Fah Weel Drive!" Idi shouted enthusiastically on the steeper sections of the ride, a reference to his firm belief that camels could go places that no Land Rover could get close to visiting.

By midafternoon, the heat was unbearable. All five of us clients asked Idi to take us back to camp, as that seemed to be the only place within 500 miles that offered any kind of shade (trees in Kenya have thorns, not leaves). We were deposited back on the riverbank, and started in on the crate of beer again. The heat was horrific.

After an hour of inactivity, Benny jumped to his feet. "I'm so fricking hot!" he said, eyeing the gravely dirt of the riverbed. "I'm going to build a bathtub!"

Benny picked up a shovel that was among our camp supplies, and wandered down to the legendary river, or legendary riverbed as the case was this time. Selecting a point in the middle of the parched expanse, he began digging. Within 15 minutes, he had excavated a hole in the riverbed, and brown, filthy water began seeping into the cavity. Benny dug a little more, until the hole was approximately six feet by three feet, and about 18 inches deep. Then, to the surprise of the proper British ladies sitting in the shade on the bank and sipping beer, Benny stripped off all his clothes and climbed into the murky pit. He scooped the filthy brown water up and dumped it on his head.

"Oh my!" said Moira, the Scottish woman. "What on earth is he doing?"

"I can't believe he's doing that!" said Jenny, one of the English girls. "That's disgusting!"

I laughed out loud, got out of my chair, and went down to the riverbed to watch the spectacle from closer range. Sitting naked in a hole that was barely up to his buttocks, Benny was sloshing brown water over all parts of his body. The water, we both noticed, was filled with small, spherical goat turds that were, apparently, a main ingredient in the sandy, gravely material that constituted the river bottom.

Consider the bathtub. It is by far one of humankind's greatest inventions, and the bath one of his greatest activities. What other water-borne event combines soothing heat, deep relaxation and incredible between-the-folds cleansing? Of course, humans have been using bathtubs for millennia.

They were common in ancient Rome, Greece, Crete, Egypt and Babylon. The invention and refinement of the device closely follows that of civilizations in arid regions, where it was necessary to control, ration and conserve water. (By comparison, my hairy heathen ancestors in northern Britain likely wanted little to do with baths—they were constantly drenched from rain, mud, snow, slush and more rain.)

Anyway, according to *Plumbing and Mechanical Magazine*, "by 2500 B.C. the Egyptians were pretty adept with drainage construction, accentuated by the significance that water played in their priestly rituals of purification and those affecting the burial of the kings. According to their religion, to die was simply to pass from one state of life to another. If the living required food, clothing and other accouterments of daily life, so did the dead. Thus, it's not surprising that archaeologists have discovered bathrooms in some tombs."

The Latin term *plumbus,* from which we get our modern words plumbing and plumber, means lead. (*Plumbus butt* comes galloping to mind at this point, but I dare say it has morphed over time). Roman plumbers were lead artisans whose job it was to build or repair any apparatus associated with water distribution. The occupation was important in ancient Rome—so important that the term has persisted to this day.

Although most ancient civilizations in arid areas invented their own plumbing systems and bathing apparatuses, it was the Romans who communized the activity with the great baths. Few human group activities are as ingrained in the psyche as the Roman bath. They were the ancient equivalents of country clubs. One paid a small entrance fee, and then went inside where it was possible to exercise in a gym, recreate, dine and, of course, spend time in a vast array of baths ranging from cold to tepid to warm to scalding. At first, Roman baths were conservative, single-sex affairs—men here, women there. As time progressed, however, and various emperors came and went, bathhouse rules were relaxed, leading to multi-sex bathing facilities and a lot of 1980s porno filmmakers' fantasies.

As Benny sloshed about in his hole in the stark nakedness of the Ewaso Ngiro River Valley, I laughed hard. If the Roman communal bath was the highest bathing ideal, then this had to be the low point.

"Aww, those Brits are so friggin' uptight," he said smiling at me, and picking a small round turd out of the water and flicking it into the air. "At least I'm staying cool. Just call me Bwana Fisis."

Water quality in Africa has always been a big worry for me, and while

Benny sloshed about, I ran off to get one of our travel guidebooks.

"Let's see," I said, standing over Benny and flipping through several pages, "What can possibly be passed through water or insects that live in water? Bilharzia might have some potential here. Little worms that get into your intestines and bladder. Spread by freshwater snails. This place should be full of 'em. Trypanosomiasis is another prize-winner. Passed along by tsetse flies. Is that a tsetse fly on your shoulder? Then of course, there's various forms of dysentery, hepatitis, fungal infections, malaria, giardia, typhoid, worms … Jeez, Benny, the list goes on and on."

Benny glared at me: "Do you mind? I'm taking my bath!"

I reached in and felt the water. Although horribly dirty, it was cool and extremely inviting. I grabbed the shovel and was soon sitting besides Benny in a bathtub of my own. We spent the rest of the day sipping beer and wallowing, literally, in cool, refreshing muck. Our British colleagues tried to ignore us.

Anthony returned to camp early on the fourth day, on foot. "Guys," he said plaintively, "You're not going to believe this but… "

The story he told us was simply crazy, yet it seemed to fit in perfectly with our safari to date. While driving back to a nearby village to get the tire fixed, Anthony had gotten another flat. He had no spare, so he hitchhiked his way back to the village, where he spent the night with a Samburu family. In the morning, he had arranged some help and, with several local mechanics, had driven out to retrieve the truck. Then, after fixing both tires, he had driven it back towards Camp One. On the way, he got another flat. Finally—ditching the truck, which was now gathering dust on the side of the road somewhere—Anthony had returned to Camp One on foot to update us on the situation.

"Is everyone having a good time?" he asked.

We all answered in the affirmative, then Anthony, grabbing a handful of food from the camp kitchen, started jogging back up the road: "I'm going to try and get the truck sorted out. I'll be back tonight. If you see Malcolm, don't tell him where I am, okay?" We promised not to, and Anthony bounded off through the scrub. I wondered if Kenya's long-distance runners started out as camel safari supervisors.

We spent the morning of our fourth safari day riding camels in loops around Camp One, and scratching several layers of skin off our arms on the thorny trees. By noon, Benny and I were ready for a dip.

While Idi, the three British women, and the camp cooks fussed over lunch, Benny and I went down to the riverbed. We dug the bathtubs out a little, stripped off, and sat. Soon, Moira and the two English girls came down to the river for a closer examination, each holding a bottle of our beer.

"You know boys" said Moira, in her aristocratic Scots, "We girls have been thinking. It's awfully hot, and we would really like to cool off a bit. Would you mind if we tried out your, ahem—she cleared her throat—baths?"

Fifteen minutes later, Benny and I sat in the lawn chairs next to camp and watched as three uptight British socialites immersed themselves in the murky, fetid brown, shit-festooned waters of the Ewaso Ngiro.

The rest of the week floated by in much the same fashion. Idi would take us camel riding in the morning, and by midafternoon, when it was too hot to be in the sun, we'd take turns sitting in riverbottom bathtubs in the dried-out riverbed. We polished off the rest of the second beer crate and diligently improved our tubs when their walls caved in. At one point, three Samburu morans strolled past camp, on their way to somewhere. They noticed us sitting in the holes in the riverbed. They seemed to like the idea, and after we had left, they slipped in and enjoyed a cool refreshing soak.

Figuring that demand was rising, Benny and I built several additional tubs—big tubs, for communal dips, such as the women took; small tubs for those seeking privacy; deep bathtubs for really cooling down; and shallow ones for a quick splash. By about 3 o'clock on any given day, at least half a dozen people could be found lounging about in our bathtubs, lolling in filthy water, sipping Tusker Beer, and trying not to think about the hot African sun which was slowly roasting our brains.

On our second to last safari day, Anthony decided we should move camp, in order to see a little more of the local scenery. He had the truck working again, and with the delicacy of a military advance, we abandoned Camp One for Camp Two.

Camp Two wasn't really Camp Two, of course. It was just a spot near some high eucalyptus trees about a kilometer "downstream" from Camp One, nowhere near the 15 to 18 kilometers we were supposed to be traveling between overnight stops. Camp Two was less shaded, and by about midday, we were all crouching around the trunk of a tree trying to escape the piercing sun. The flies were worse and the riverbed was mostly rock, almost impossible for digging. Still, Benny managed to scratch a new bathtub out of the rocky gravel.

The biggest tragedy of Camp Two was, however, the simple fact that we'd run out of beer, and as sundown approached, we wondered how we would survive a sober night on this most bizarre of excursions. Much agitated discussion followed lunch that afternoon, especially since Anthony had left with the truck again, to go repair another flat tire. Idi, sensing an emergency, asked me for five Kenyan shillings (about a nickel), and wandered off to visit several nearby *manyattas*, small compounds in which Samburus live, generally consisting of one to three woven huts. They are surrounded by a thick wall of tangled thorn branches, designed to keep lions, hyenas and other dangerous creatures out. Out-of-control safaris too, I dare say.

At the third manyatta he visited, Idi was able to buy some *changaa*, putrid, home-fermented liquor made, I'm guessing, out of vegetable scraps. Idi arrived back in camp that night sometime after dinner, carrying the changaa in a plastic, yellow, one-gallon vegetable oil bottle that still had a lot of vegetable oil on its side, top and bottom. He took several swigs of the clear, curious liquid, then passed the bottle to Moira.

"Acck!" she said, waving it away. "No thank you, Idi! That is foul!"

My turn came, and, wanting to show Idi, Matthew and Mbundo I was one of the boys, I took a large, hearty swig. My throat burned and my stomach churned. Changaa tasted remarkably like gasoline, and felt about as good going down. I passed the bottle onto Benny, who took a sip and then said, "Mmmm, that's enough for me!" No one else wanted any either, but that was fine with Idi, and as the evening slipped by, he was able to finish the entire gallon. Unfortunately, no Sammy Davis lounge songs were forthcoming.

Our last day arrived and we went for a short camel ride in the morning, followed by a minimalist lunch of cabbage and rice. We were, apparently, running low on food. Anthony, who was still MIA, had arranged to pick us up in the truck around noon. As we found out later, the truck had gotten another flat and Anthony was walking somewhere between Camp Two and the small village yet again, no doubt pondering his future employment options.

Idi suggested we ride the camels back to Marallal, a sort of self-rescue, if it could be called that. After two hours of rough country, thousands of thorny trees and much blood loss, we came across a dirt road. We followed that for another hour, until, finally, off in the distance, Idi spotted a plume of yellow dust: "Anthony come!"

We left the camels with Matt and Mbundo, said a fond farewell to the two young warriors, and loaded ourselves into the truck. Twenty minutes up the road, the truck's rear right wheel began wobbling. "No problem!" Anthony said flooring the vehicle. But it was no use, the truck began vibrating wildly, and he had to pull over. We all piled out of the truck to inspect the damage.

"No good!" Idi said dramatically, pointing to the rotor, the fat metal disk to which the wheel is attached. "Broke!"

"Really, Idi?" Moira said. "You're very perceptive. Marallal University of neurophysics, perhaps?"

A flat—dozens of them, for that matter—had been no big deal. A busted rotor was another matter. Anthony, Idi, Benny and I jacked the truck up and removed the wheel. Several lug bolts had been stripped off the rotor, and those that were still attached were bent and mangled. We waited on the side of the deserted road and flagged every car, bus and truck that went past. Nearly everyone who came along stopped, but could neither help us with fixing our vehicle, nor a ride back to Marallal. In Africa, if a vehicle is going somewhere, so are the dozens of local people who can squeeze inside it. We pulled out camp sleeping pads sat on the rocky ground at the side of the road.

Then came the bees. Not just any bees mind you, but African bees. You know, the so-called killer bees that swarm and sting their enemies to death. Anthony first noticed the bees as he was trying to remove the bathtub shovel from the back of the truck. "Idi!" he called to the Samburu camel guide. "Bees! Bees! Bees!"

Idi—who I'd guessed was crazy, and this proved it—climbed up into the truck, took off his pink, dress-like robe, and began swatting at the bees. The bees buzzed loudly and quickly grew in number. But that didn't seem to bother Idi. He kept swatting and the bees kept swarming.

Anthony grabbed an old cardboard carton that was stashed among the gear in the back of the truck. He took out a cigarette lighter, set the cardboard alight, and dropped the burning box on the floor of the truck. He then grabbed a burlap sack, and dumped this on top of the burning box. Idi kept swatting and I grabbed my video camera to record the weird melée. The entire truck filled with smoke, and the safari clients sitting on the roadside moved back 20 feet, just in case the entire vehicle burst into flame. It didn't, and after 30 minutes the bees were under control. So, luckily, was the fire. But the vehicle was still going nowhere.

A short time after the rotor breakdown/bee attack/fire melée, Moira broke down. Everyone on the safari—staffers and clients alike—knew the older woman was going to crack, but we had been praying that she'd hold it together until we got back to Marallal. She couldn't and she began screaming, telling our African hosts what she thought of them and their safari, and how she was going to kill Malcolm. It wasn't pretty, and, as soon as another vehicle approached, Anthony flagged it down and pushed Moira inside.

"I will be fired," Anthony said glumly. "But at least she has gone. She made me crazy."

Sadly, we all guessed Anthony's prediction would later come true. Ironically, it had been Malcolm's own lack of trust in both Anthony and other Africans that led to Anthony's demise. He hadn't given Anthony the spare tires he needed for such rough country. But on the other hand, Malcolm wasn't an idiot. What self-respecting businessman, who had seen dozens of spare tires stolen from his trucks over the years, would offer up an endless supply to the very same people—local Africans—that had been stealing them? The African struggle for European respect—just like the European regard for their native hosts—was beaten down by the grim realities of the Kenyan bush.

Around sunset, five hours after the rotor breakdown/bee attack/fire melée, we were met by a friendly Kikuyu driver, operating a spanking new minibus. "Marallal, anyone?" he asked with a smile. We climbed inside the small white van and sat silently, staring wide-eyed at the road in the minibus's headlights while we were transported back to Yare Safaris world headquarters. None of us actually believed we'd get there.

By the time we arrived, Moira, of course, was in the bar, drinking and demanding Malcolm's head on a plate. Benny, Jenny, Sally and I arrived and also asked to see Malcolm. Not surprisingly, he wasn't there. According to the bartender, Malcolm was in Nairobi. And, the bartender told us, perhaps to solicit a little sympathy in the face of an angry crowd, Malcolm was sick. Moira explained to the bartender that we were going to do some drinking at his expense. Malcolm owed me $20 for paying for a couple of the flats, and he owed Benny a goat—a goat Benny had paid for a traditional Samburu ceremony, which had been sneaked out of camp and eaten by our camel wranglers.

Twenty dollars' worth of Tusker later—which, in Africa, is a lot—I stumbled off to bed. In the morning, Benny and I once again loaded ourselves into the minibus behind the three British women, and we began our long, rough trip back to Nairobi. The sun was blazing, and we rolled all the windows down.

The five of us recalled the previous week's events, and tried to figure out exactly why it had been such a disaster. A drought was blamed for the dry river; a British expatriate was to blame for our lack of transport and a single camp tour; Idi's lack of tender, white skin was to blame for our miserable camel rides through the acacia trees; and we were all to blame for signing up in the first place.

Back in our Nairobi hotel, I was packing for our trip home when I came across a brochure describing the wild, thrilling, outrageous, once-annual Marallal International Camel Derby. I showed it to Benny—Marallal was already calling us back.

'ON' THE 'ROAD'

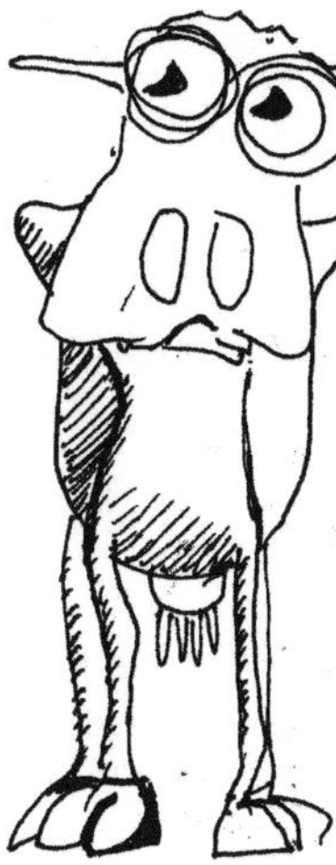

Holy Cows and Traffic Jams

(India, 1999)

"In Australia, cows and sheep are responsible for about 90 percent of methane emissions in the agriculture sector, producing 3,000,000 tonnes of methane each year. Other sources are fossil fuel extraction, waste disposal and natural sources such as wetlands and termites. Most of the methane comes from livestock burps, with animal wastes a small source. A typical cow burps 280 liters of methane daily as a result of microbial digestion of fodder in its stomach. Sheep produce about 25 liters of methane each day."

—"Livestock Burp into the Headlines," *Labonline.com.au*

There are a lot of cities on earth that rank up there in terms of worst traffic. Large cities in Europe are known for their angst-ridden drivers who whip through miniature streets at lightning speeds. African roads are filled with overloaded *matatus* (minivans) that regularly careen off highways in the countryside killing dozens of people a week. And Latin American drivers are famous for their laissez-faire attitudes toward road rules and an unwavering penchant for bribing the cops. Over the years, I've managed to visit and study a few of these traffic black holes with a mixture of amazement, awe and relief before returning home only to wonder who has the worst traffic on earth. Then I went to India and was enlightened.

In late 1999 I managed to land a job photographing a footrace through the Himalayan foothills of West Bengal, one of the exotic eastern states of India jutting up between Bhutan and Nepal like a hitchhiker's thumb along a West Texas highway. I tagged along as runners from a dozen nations chugged their way along the India-Nepal border for five days, running 13 to 20 miles a day at elevations close to 12,000 feet. Some barfed, some bled, some swore off marathon running for good. Some fell down and scraped their knees and kept running. One fell down and broke his nose and kept running! Running, I learned, is serious business—made me glad I was doing photography.

I spent the week taking pictures with an English journalist named Steve Goodwin. Our days were a mixture of riding Jeeps to get in front of the fastest runners, then hiking for miles to follow and photograph the slower folks. Throw in several dozen tea stops with friendly Sherpa people, a backdrop that included Mt. Everest, Kanchenjunga, Makalu and other stunning peaks, and we're talking about a pretty decent job in one of the world's most beautiful locations. (Predictably, the pay sucked.) But, in all honesty, gazing out across the beautiful Himalayas, I was slightly depressed. At some point, this idyllic jaunt into the high hills would come to an end and I'd end up back down on the Indian flatlands, in a big city, dealing with that crazy Indian traffic. I hung my head and tried not to think about it. I wanted to stay high.

If you've ever been to India, you probably noticed the traffic. Like me, your first reaction to it was probably something like "Man, this is nuts!" Your second reaction might've been along the lines of "I didn't know driving could be an art form!" And, your third reaction was probably pretty close to "Doing tricks on my skateboard here is definitely out of the question!"

When you analyze Indian traffic on a more scientific level, you get a pretty good understanding of how Indians think, how they live, how they commute and, most important of all, how they worship. But to analyze Indian traffic, you must first break it down into its multiple parts. High up in the Himalayan foothills with only a few Jeeps around is an excellent place to begin that breaking-down process. (Breaking down having multiple meanings in my case.)

Problem Number One is the exhaust. The typical Indian vehicle seems to have absolutely no system for cleaning air as it leaves the tailpipe; no catalytic converters, no mesh screens, no charcoal filters, no slurry piles, no roadblocks, no Hoover Dams—nothing that might keep the engine from expelling thousands of pounds of caustic carcinogenic waste into the pristine sky with every revolution of the engine. The Jeeps we were using in the high mountain air were extreme examples of this. Some of the runners we drove along in front of while taking photos nearly killed us, and we them.

Because these Jeeps needed to carry more-than-normal amounts of fuel, oftentimes gasoline drums with said extra fuel were carried in the back seat. Our particular drum leaked and dripped all over my shoes, and the fumes burned the inner walls of our nostrils. Now multiply that single stinky, noisy, high-mountain Jeep by the several hundred million vehicles down on the flatlands, and you'll begin to understand what a big city in India smells like: a coal-fired power plant with an auxiliary diesel refinery on the roof on a bad day. No, wait: every coal-fired power plant on earth having a collective bad day.

Problem Number Two is the number and mix of vehicles. My first day on the subcontinent was spent roaming around Old and New Delhi, two cities separated by name and time, but together forming one giant mass of humanity. On any given day, all of Delhi's tens of millions of people seem to be going somewhere. They walk, pedal bicycles, ride in rickshaws, steer horse-drawn carts, hire taxis, and hop on scooters to get where they're going. These different transportation mediums are all mixed together on the street, weaving in and out like the strands of a complex tapestry. To see the various forms of travel in an Indian streetscape takes time. You have to study. Layer upon layer of moving humanity cannot be absorbed in an instant. The problem—or rather, potential problem—that this mix presents should be fairly obvious: just picture spokes versus rumps, legs versus truck wheels, steel versus flesh. You get the idea.

The most amazing vehicle I saw was a human torso. It was in Old Delhi, and I noticed it out the side of our taxi. There, in one of the city's busiest streets, was a middle-aged man who was missing both his legs from the groin down. At first I thought he was a body, a badly mutilated body resulting from a car accident. His white clothes—rags, really—were sort of wrapped around his lower body, the stump end of him. When I first noticed him, he was squatting on the edge of the street, looking at the mix and depth of traffic. (Leprosy doesn't just affect India's children, and it doesn't just take fingers and toes. Many of the estimated six million who suffer from leprosy lose half their body. This man was in a bad way.) I watched for a moment, feeling the most extreme sense of sadness I've ever felt.

While I was deep in self-assessment, this man started rolling. Writhing like a fish out of water, he propelled his abdomen to turn over on the street. It was his method of travel, the way one of us might roll over in bed. He rolled over and over, at times quite quickly, weaving through an ocean of cars, motorcycles, scooters, rickshaws, bicycles, and humans on foot. Rush-hour walkers and drivers were careful to step over and swerve around him,

but he was so adroit at rolling that he was quicker than the surrounding traffic. Indeed, he was as quick as a trout in a Rocky Mountain stream. The man rolled up against a grungy gutter, below a street vendor selling chunks of coconut, and stopped on his belly. He arched his back, bringing his face up squarely in front of the vendor, and held out his hand for a coin. The vendor waved him away with a dirty look. The Torso Man rolled back out into the traffic. We swerved past, and I couldn't see him anymore. His was the most unique vehicle I'm sure I'll ever see.

On the subcontinent, the roads are another challenge.

Everywhere, they seem to be either in terrible disrepair or so overburdened by non-transportation-related activities so as to make them unusable. In other words, non-vehicular things are plonked down in the road because there's no room anywhere else. Street vendors are the most notorious. Since the sidewalks in India are generally nonexistent, pedestrians tend to walk along the edge of the street. The street vendors—who sell everything from corn on the cob to stereos and shoes—move onto the edge of the street, so they are closer to the pedestrian bypassers. I guess the vendors figure that the closer they are to the foot traffic, the closer they are to a sale. The creeping infringement means there's little room left for cars, trucks, bicycles, horse-drawn carts, my friend the Torso Man, and whatever else might be actually using the street for movement.

In the Darjeeling area in the Himalayan foothills, where the running event was staged, the roads have a different problem. They are so twisted and steep that an as-the-crow-flies journey of five miles might take four hours and cover 30 miles. And because the roads are so steep and twisted, drivers must take most corners blindly. That means laying on the horn as one sweeps through a turn. For the entire drive back from the race, I sat shuddering in the back of a Jeep while our driver—presumably showing off his chauffeuring skills—tried to set a new speed record for the three-hour drive from Mirik to Bagdogra. I felt like I was in a horror movie about a circus.

Lastly, I have to mention the noise. Years ago, some Indian motorist must have decided he was having a hard time keeping track of where the cars around him were (he probably had bad eyesight), so he decided to paint "Sound Horn" across the back of his car. You know, a friendly little toot-toot to warn him that, indeed, a giant lorry is about to flatten his little Mini or Whatever-it-was he was driving. A second Indian driver must've decided, "Hey, what a great idea"—because, of course, other vehicles were making their presence known. So the second driver, forgetting what the first driver had painted on his car, goes home and paints "Blow Horn" across the trunk. The idea spread, paint went on and today every single vehicle in India has either "Blow Horn" or "Sound Horn" painted across the back of the vehicle in big encouraging letters. And because Indians are such neighborly types, everyone blows his horn, all the time, all day and all night. The sound is deafening.

All these parts—the fumes, the smell, the mix of transportation devices, the roads, the drivers, the noise—go a long way toward helping India get to the top of the Bad Traffic charts, but if there's one single factor that keeps India at the number one spot, I'd have to vote for the cows. Yep, cows. Those harmless, brainless docile beasts we pump full of antibiotics, milk 'til their udders fall off and sledgehammer for hamburgers. Cows.

I first noticed India's cows in New Delhi, along the sides of the wide boulevards, in the gardens built in roundabouts, and wandering through various human markets. They lived unmolested, side-by-side with their fellow, street-dwelling humans. They seemed to be better fed than a lot of the people and appeared a lot happier.

After my photographic jaunt to the hills for the race, I took a four-day tour of central India: Agra, home of the Taj Mahal, and the Rajasthan city of Jaipur, the Pink City. In Agra and Jaipur, the cows congregate on the two-foot-wide concrete medians separating the lanes of traffic. That they could even sit on these low, skinny walls of concrete is surprising. That the pulsing mass of traffic doesn't smash one of the cows into oblivion is astonishing.

"That would not be a good thing," said my driver, Raj Kumaar, as we wove in and out of Jaipur's crowded streets. "To a Hindu, to hit a cow, that would be a bad thing. A very bad thing."

"But why not move these cows off the streets?" I asked. "They're damn dangerous."

"Ah, but they are lifegivers," Raj said. "They bring milk and cheese.

We must let them live happily and peacefully."

As Raj spoke, we drove past a cow whose horns were painted green. I pointed, and raised my eyebrows in the rearview mirror at her.

"That is a sign of respect," he said.

We skidded around the green-horned cow, wiped out several bicyclists, and continued on our way.

In India, the cow has more political clout that the Prime Minister's secretary. Indian bovinity goes back over 4,000 years, as early inhabitants of the subcontinent worshiped the bull as a fertility symbol. In later years, the Hindu religion's nonviolent, vegetarian credo meant that dairy products became the primary source of protein. Additionally, the animal was a source of energy on a continent where most carbon-powered machinery is either too costly or simply not available. When castrated, a bull provides Indian farmers with a reliable beast of burden. It pulls the plow, takes products to market, eats leftover fodder and endures the long hot Indian summers and the torrential monsoons easily. (Of course, the real benefit to cows is that they are a transport device that won't push the Indian atmosphere to some kind of breaking point in terms of air pollution.) Anyway, it's no wonder the cow became a symbol of wealth and one of Hinduism's most prevalent icons. But that's not to say cow worship—and the resultant traffic mess—is necessarily a good thing.

A lot of the cows in India are poor milk producers and of no use to humans, but they remain wandering the streets, pooping everywhere and causing occasional automobile accidents. In the mid-1960s, the human population of India was 500 million, and another 12.5 million people were being born annually. The cattle population was estimated at 250 million, with a lot of that number being of the "tired-and-sick" variety. Today, the numbers are a little different (one billion people and around 200 million cows), but the issue remains a big one.

In a poignant essay in *The World Paper* in 1998, Associate Editor Amitabha Chowdhury wrote: "Despite these grim realities, after 30 years of cow politics their slaughter is still prohibited in all but three states in India. The leather industry's procurement agents must stay on the fringes, and wait either for a clandestine deal or the demise of the cow. As with the issue of population control, whether or not to slaughter cows remains a battle ground between the modernists, who favor the much-needed reform, and the revivalists, who warn the voter against either measure."

I continued my Indian tour, taking in the stunning forts of Jaipur, and the Taj Mahal in Agra, watching as history and humanity mixed on the street with potential hamburgers.

I'll admit, I like cows. I always have. I'm not the only one. I recently did a web search on cow facts and came up with a whopping 120,000 web pages that included or were devoted entirely to information about cows. And these pages have some really odd information, begging the question, who is your typical cow enthusiast?

To wit, I will quote a few:

• "A cow stands up and sits down about 14 times a day;

• "The oldest cow ever recorded was a dremon named Big Bertha that died three months shy of her 49th birthday on New Year's Eve, 1993. Big Bertha also holds the record for lifetime breeding as she produced 39 calves;

• "In the ancient Celtic religion, a black cow symbolizes death;

• "The highest milk yield for a single day is an unbelievable 241 pounds by a cow named Urbe Blanca;

• "Dairy cows can produce 125 pounds of saliva a day;

• "A 1,000-pound cow produces an average of ten tons of manure a year;

• "Cows have 12 large back molars in each jaw, and eight incisors located on the bottom jaw, and a thick pad on the top jaw;

• "The greatest yield for one lactation (365 days) is 59,298 pounds by a Holstein cow named Robthom Suzet Paddy;

• "It takes 400 liters of blood to flow through the udder to produce one liter of milk;

• "In 1930, the first cow to fly was Elm Farm Ollie, who was milked in an airplane;

• "The heaviest live birth of a calf is 225 pounds for a British Friesian cow in 1961;

• "The highest lifetime yield of milk for a single cow is 465,224 pounds by the creatively-named cow No. 289;

• "Dairy cows can produce up to 200 pounds of flatus (farts and burps) a day."

These tidbits appeared to have been offered up by mostly American and European cow lovers, and there are millions of them. (Prompting a better question—whatever happened to names like Bossie? Bertha and Elm Farm Ollie are okay, but Urbe Blanca? And Robthom Suzet Paddy? What are these dairy farmers smoking?) Anyway, we Westerners might like cows but the Hindus have us beat by a mile.

Cows are so important to Hindus that—according to a news report I recently read—one Hindu couple in Singapore brought a cow and a calf up to their new high-rise apartment via elevator (not to mention 40 relatives) in order to bless the home in a traditional ceremony. Renting the cow cost the couple a whopping $480, but there was an extra $200 in cleaning bills after the cow crapped in the living room during the ceremony!

It wasn't until I made it back to Delhi where the holy cows really made an impression. It was rush hour, on a weekday, and I'd been out with a government-loaned driver named Sundeep checking out the Red Fort, one of Old Delhi's most significant landmarks. On the way back to my hotel, on one of New Delhi's biggest and grandest boulevards, we got caught up in a blitzkrieg of vehicles. It was bumper-to-bumper, curb-to-curb, wall-to-wall; so tight I could've licked the car next to me. Everyone and everything was humming along at a solid 40 miles per hour, until suddenly, the entire mess came to a grinding halt. I heard the shattering of glass and the unmistakable sound of metal buckling and tearing. Apparently no one was hurt, it was just a mild fender-bender somewhere along the temporary steel snake behind us. But we weren't going anywhere either.

We sat, waited and watched. Tempers rose, while Sikh drivers (the most notorious in India) yelled at each other from taxis. Then, after several minutes of nothing, we watched a white car up ahead of us jostle a few feet one direction. It was trying to get around some kind of obstacle, but was so far ahead of us that we couldn't tell what the object might be. Then the white car began slowly moving away from the mess, heading up the street, gaining speed as it departed the jam until we couldn't see it any longer. The rickshaw beside the white car did the same thing, pulling itself from the automotive quagmire slowly, then speeding off into the distance. One by one, cars ahead of us meticulously inched their way around something up ahead, before resuming normal cruising speed for New Delhi's Ashok Road at 5:30 p.m. on a Wednesday. The slight movement in the near pileup crept towards us. With anticipation, we tried to see the thing that had caused the entire traffic jam. I was sure there was going to be a pile of human and vehicular remains with someone important inside. Finally, we were upon it. But, as you probably guessed, it was a cow. The thing was slowly

wandering southbound in a never-ending stream of automobiles that were heading north. One by one, drivers carefully worked their vehicles around the beast, then sped off into the evening. This particular cow didn't care one bit about the heavy traffic—she was happily meandering along, indiscriminantly changing lanes and breaking all sorts of road rules.

In Chowdhury's essay, he argues that India's holy cows have retarded the nation's agricultural and economic growth, and goes on to point out that the Indian buffalo produces better quality and more milk than cows, its mortality rate is low, and it is by and large a cheaper creature to sustain. "The bovine burden on India's back will continue," he concludes, "sustained by India's veneration of the cow and sad indifference towards the buffalo."

So, although many modern Indians like Chowdhury are challenging the ancient and almost ridiculous veneration of the cow for the economy's sake, I think they're missing the real point—rush hour. Because of these revered cows, India has the worst traffic in the world. Hands down, drop dead, bar none, period! Nothing beats the place.

Sure, no question the fumes, the smell, the mix of transportation devices, the roads, the drivers, the noise—all that stuff—contributes to getting India near the top of the list. But all countries have those things to some degree. It's all those things plus these holy cows that gives India the edge.

On my home computer, I have a video game called *Carmageddon 2: Carpocalypse Now* (My wife is hiding her face in her palms as I type this). In *Carpocalypse Now*, one drives around smashing into things: buildings, cars, pedestrians, dogs, other racers. It comes with a game player's manual, *The Max Damage Offensive Driving School Student Handbook*. Whenever I need a break from my work as a writer, I crank up *Carmageddon 2*, (turn off the dogs on the controls) and let my mind go in a weird, evil rush of adrenaline. I don't know much about the manufacturers of *Carmageddon*, SCI (Sales Curve Interactive), and whether or not they have plans for *Carmageddon 3*, but I bet *Carmageddon In India* would be the most difficult video game ever conceived.

Needless to say, you'd hear players muttering a few "Holy Cows."

Dribbling Across the Elk Mountains: The Wilderness World Cup

(Colorado, 1998)

"What's the sense in all this?"
—Warren Harding, *Downward Bound*

The summer of 1998 was a strange one, at least in terms of weather. Meteorologists said that the continental United States was suffering from a post-El Niño weather phenomenon known as La Niña, and predicted several weather patterns as a result. Around Colorado, it manifested itself in long periods of extremely hot, dry weather, punctuated by multiday periods of monsoon-like downpours.

In early July, my wife and I, along with two friends, undertook a four-day trek through the Hunter-Fryingpan Wilderness, a remote, little-known area of high mountains and swampy river valleys just west of the Continental Divide. It rained on us every day, and by the time we reached the trailhead at the upper end of the Fryingpan Valley, we were ready for home. I was determined not to venture out again. But a few days later, a friend and neighbor, Bob Ward, called and asked if I was interested in another four-day trek, this time through the Maroon Bells-Snowmass Wilderness Area, a wilderness area directly south of my Basalt, Colorado, home.

Although I had just returned from a soggy wilderness trek, I was eager to go. For one thing, Bob was moving away. He and I, along with our wives, had taken dozens of trips together to mountainous regions in Colorado we wanted to explore. We had shared many fine summer evenings over barbecued dinners. And we had relied on each other for canine care, when one or the other of our families was going out of town. The other reason was that I wanted to traverse the Maroon Bells-Snowmass Wilderness Area. As is so often the case with many of us who live in and around ski resorts, we never seem to bother with exploring our own back yards.

As we prepared for our trek, I got a wild idea. I had recently been rejected from entering Tahiti by the French government because of my Australian citizenship and was nursing a sort of personal anti-France grudge. For the most part, this campaign was manifested in my switching to California wines (which are better anyway), and not eating truffles (which I didn't do anyway, although the statement of boycott sounded good). When the French won the 1998 World Cup soccer tournament over the highly favored Brazilian team, I was incensed. So, I asked myself, what could I do to out-soccer the French? What could I do to show French soccer stars like Emmanuel Petit, Laurent Blanc and Zinadine Zidane that they weren't the most talented dribblers on earth. Dribbling a soccer ball across 15 miles of rugged mountains in Central Colorado was a sure, albeit demented, bet.

Some of the greatest moments in exploration and adventure have had little to do with finding one particular point than they have with passing through a whole region, i.e., the grand traverse. Ferdinand Magellan (1480-1521) is considered one of history's greatest navigators not because he discovered the Pacific Ocean, but because he (well, his crew—he was killed in the Phillipines) made the first circumnavigation of Mother Earth, proving among other things that the world is round.

British explorer Eric Shipton (1907-1977) is considered by many mountaineers one of the sport's greatest. Not because he lay the foundations for the first ascent of Mt. Everest in 1953 by leading a decade's worth of exploratory teams there to find a feasible route up the mountain, but because he almost single-handedly developed the small, lightweight expedition ethic. His extensive traverses through portions of the Himalayas, the Patagonian Andes and various East African ranges stand as a tribute less to finding points than to passing through.

Late 1990s attempts to circle the globe by millionaire Steve Fossett in a hot-air balloon likewise feature the completion of a long journey as the achievement. The flying to one particular point on the map or other is almost trivial. Or pointless, rather.

So, when Bob and Elizabeth picked me up for the ride to the trailhead, I explained my pointless plan—to dribble a number four soccer ball from the southern trailhead in Lead King Basin near the tiny town of Marble through to thc Snowmass Creek trailhead, on the northern side of the wilderness area near the town of Basalt. Over high mountain passes, across streams and rivers, over snowfields and across scree slopes, all without ever touching the ball with my hands.

Neither Bob nor Elizabeth thought I was serious. It was too whacky, even for these creative, uninhibited people. But, as always, they just let me do my thing and laughed out loud when I produced a tartan cap with tufts of fake red hair attached to it: "It ain't a soccer match without a few soccer hooligans along!" I said, explaining that the rowdiest hooligans were the Scots.

After we had dumped our packs on the roadside high above Marble, Bob rode back along the rough four-wheel-drive road for several miles with Elizabeth, to make sure she would be able to get the truck over some particularly nasty sections of road. I picked up my pack, slung it over my shoulder, then wound my foot back and let fly with a loud whump. The ball flew up into the air, then bounced across some grass and came to rest in some weeds, ten yards away. I hiked over to it, and kicked again. Another whump, and another ten yards. I continued up a small hill where the road petered out as it came to the trailhead, at the very edge of the wilderness. Since Bob was still with Elizabeth, I decided to descend to our drop-off point and ferry his pack up to the wilderness edge. I waited around for 15 minutes, hoping that Bob would return and photograph the ball's first touch on this epic and historic journey. Half an hour later, when Bob still hadn't turned up, I booted the ball up the trail and the game (ding-ding) was underway.

I dribbled the ball while ferrying the packs for about a half-mile up the gently sloping trail. For the most part, it was easy work. The sides of the trail were lined with three-foot-tall weeds, so the ball had a sort of gutter to roll along inside. Every 30 feet or so, I'd take a nice swing and punt it with my toe; the ball would rise, then drop, usually inside the grass gutter, then roll along a few more feet before coming to rest on an incongruity in the trail. Piece of cake, I thought.

However, 20 minutes later when Bob finally caught up with me—laughing hysterically at my antics—the vegetation along the trail was beginning to thin. We were probably around 10,000 feet in elevation, and the trail's edges were becoming rockier and rockier. Every time the ball hit a rock, it bounced wildly in all directions. To add to the challenge, the trail was contouring across a slope. There was a steep slope to our right (Meadow Mountain), and a creek-filled gully to our left (the Silver Creek drainage). Once every half dozen or so kicks, the rambunctious ball would bounce off a rock and go flying down into the gully, which meant I had to take my pack off and go dribble it out of the gully and back to the trail with my feet.

Regardless, we made good progress. By noon we were beginning the steep climb up towards a high pass between the Crystal River drainage to the south and the Avalanche Creek drainage to the north. The higher we crept up the pass, the more rugged the terrain. I kept the ball close to my feet, to prevent it from taking a long roll back down the pass. The technique worked, although had it been a real game, my teammates would've beaten me senseless and thrown my body in front of a speeding Metro for hogging the ball.

After dribbling uphill for half a mile or so, Bob and I finally neared the crest of the pass. Only 100 feet or so separated me from our first major obstacle. Unfortunately, that 100 feet was taken up by a steep snowfield, sitting squarely in the middle of the pass. I took my pack off, and placed it on a granite outcrop. Then, I began climbing a deep cleft between the outcrop and the snowfield, a sort of narrow gash that allowed me to exercise some kind of control over the ball. Near the top of the snowfield, however, disaster struck. I stumbled momentarily, fell forward onto my hands, and the evil ball slipped out between my feet. It then rolled down across the snow, bounced off a rock, and plunged some 500 feet down the pass. I sat down for a moment and nearly cried. All that work for naught. Bob—who had been gazing at the vista on the north side of the pass—wandered over and asked where the ball was. I pointed down the side we had just climbed.

"Wow," he said, "that sucks!"

"Och! Wait here," I said, dumping my pack on the ground next to Bob. "I'll be beck, laddie!"

I scrambled down the south side of the pass and found the defiant leather orb in the middle of a flat, slushy snowfield. I heartily booted it into a gully running alongside the snowfield. It bounced around a few times, then came to rest behind a cluster of rocks. I worked the thing free with my feet, and carefully started up the steepest section of the pass for a second time. As the hill steepened, it became increasingly difficult to control. At times I found myself on all fours, my palms planted in the gravel while my feet rolled the miscreant sphere, inch-by-inch, up the hill. After 20 minutes of tricky maneuvering, I had crested the divide.

"Woohoo!" I yelled, ecstatic. "One down, two to go."

"You really going to keep going?" Bob asked. "Your 'Elks Dribble' is getting pretty ambitious."

He pointed at the terrain in front of us, which made me realize just how idiotic the task I'd created for myself really was. An enormous sweeping valley—the upper Avalanche Creek drainage—dropped off below us, and swept across roughly five miles of moraines, creeks and snowfields. The terrain was a jumble of steep rises and dramatic drop-offs, all interlaced with drainages lying at impossible angles. I gazed at the landscape, taking it in on a step-by-step, kick-by-kick basis. The gray sky began to leak a light rain.

"Och laddie!" I said to myself. "What's wrong with my genes? They didn't get filtered properly from one generation to the next! I duu the damndest things sometimes."

Still, I let fly with a massive wallop and booted the ball into the air. It traced a long arc, then rolled several hundred feet down a snowfield. Bob and I loaded up our packs, and we were off. This particular downhill run—about a mile and a half—was fairly straightforward. Our line of descent followed the fall line, and keeping the ball going was pretty easy. But when we reached the bottom of the valley and began traversing, things quickly become tedious. The ball had a physicist's sense of gravity, and with each kick—no matter how big or small—would fly straight for ten yards, then hit something (a rock, a patch of dirt, Bob's head) and take off down the valley to the northwest like a frightened dove.

It became a murderous task. Constant retrieval was followed by constant loss. My legs were doing about four times the amount of travel they would have done had I simply hiked through the wilderness. The incessant rain made the scree loose and the grass slick. But I was determined to show Zinadine Zidane (France's top goal scorer in 1998) a thing or two. (Too bad he wasn't watching.)

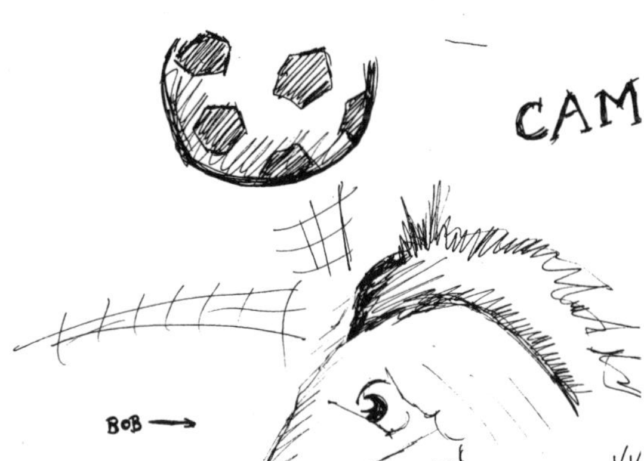

Of course, Bob is a sensible fellow, and had pretty much ignored my bizarre, neurotic soccer game from the outset. Although he had booted the ball several times in our first three miles, by the time we hit the first pass, he was content to watch, and laugh. And, he beat a fast time toward our first camp, in the Avalanche Lake area. As the afternoon progressed, I began to lag considerably behind Bob. By three p.m. he was at least a mile ahead of me. I picked up the pace of my dribbling in order to catch up.

Halfway across the upper Avalanche Creek drainage, the trail went through a swamp as it traversed the southeastern end of the valley. Although I had to walk in shin-deep, freezing water, the spastic sphere was much easier to control. With each kick, it splashed down in the tangled weeds and remained perfectly in place, until I could come along and boot it again. The bog, despite my mud-encased boots and frozen feet, was the best part of my vast dribble. The terrain remained relatively flat for a couple of miles, and the number four Mitre ball (is Mitre a French company? I had to wonder) behaved like a little angel. I even caught up with Bob, who had stopped to study a few points on the map.

"Where to next?" I asked confidently as I arrived at Bob's feet.

"It looks like the trail skirts that rocky hill, then drops into the next valley," he said, pointing north.

I studied the view grimly. The land not only became incredibly tilted (perfect for a deviant soccer ball to roll to Redstone, a town about ten miles down the valley on the northwest side of the wilderness area) but the trail—though perfectly flat—worked its way through a chaotic jumble of boulder fields. In fact, the trail was bounded on either side by rocks. One over-indulgent touch along this section of track, and it would bounce to kingdom come … or maybe even Grand Junction.

"Aye-yay-yae!" I said, wiping my brow. So far, we had come roughly five miles. Well, five miles if one followed the trail. In my nomadic-soccer-ball-shepherding trek, I'd probably covered about 20.

We continued across

the boggy flats and aimed for the chaotic jumble of boulder fields. Within a few boots of the ball, it had bounded down several hundred feet of cliff into the drainage below. I dropped my pack, and descended after it. Then, using as much patience as I could muster, I dragged the thing by my feet back up to the trail. This process, which took the better part of 15 minutes, was followed by 100 feet of dribbling along the flat trail until another pointed boulder punched my ball down the drainage again. I dumped the pack, and scrambled down the valley to retrieve it. By the time I got back, I could see Bob on the crest of the next pass, the one that would drop us down to Avalanche Lake. He stood watching me for a few minutes, then dropped out of sight.

I longed for camp. I dreamed of relaxing in the tent. I wanted to stop beating myself up on these mad scrambles to fetch the game ball, which filled my boots with rocks and mashed my shins to pulp. I wound up and booted it again. The evil orb bounded toward Redstone like the proverbial ball outta hell. It flew, jumping from boulder to boulder like a Ping-Pong ball in the weekly lottery drawing. Never had compressed air produced such an unlikely display.

I scrambled down the scree slope to search for the deviant projectile. After a solid half-hour of searching, I found it, crammed between two gigantic granite blocks that looked ready to roll on top of any probing limb that might try to retrieve the mischievous bladder. I hooked a toe over the ball, and tugged it gently. The two granite blocks stayed put, but several boulders off to one side began moving, as did the gravelly slope on which they were sitting. Within a few seconds, the ball, the hillside and myself were sliding in an uncontrolled avalanche of dirt, rocks and debris. Fortunately, it was a short ride that we all took (me, the ball, the rocks that longed for World Cup fame) before we came to a grinding halt on a flat area below the slope. I found myself sitting on a patch of grass between tall, strong pine trees. Everything was silent.

Of course, dribbling the ball back up the scree slope proved to be a complete and utter nightmare. It took a half-hour of, basically, crawling and dragging the ball by my feet. I used my hands to keep balance and to hold rolling blocks away from the ball. As the great British Himalayan explorers of the early 20th century might have observed, “It was ugly business.”

I reached the trail sometime close to dark. My nerves were shot, and my muscles were sore. It began raining again. I sat down next to my pack and eyed the trail ahead. More of the same. After a few minutes rest, I set to work anyway, doing everything humanly possible to keep the spastic projectile from launching again. In the end, my concentration was my undoing. Inching along the flat trail, I was so intent on studying the snowfield that lay ahead that I didn't notice when the ball slipped between my feet and began bouncing away. It bounced madly, like a stuck balloon, bouncing like you've never seen a ball bounce—bouncing the way pigs will, when they fly. Within a few high-speed seconds, my wilderness World Cup was over.

I sat down on my pack and almost wept. Everything I'd worked so hard for had resulted in this horrifying defeat. The final line of Shakespeare's most dramatic play, "Romeo and Juliet," came into my head: "The End."

And so it was. I hadn't the mental fortitude to flail down another quarter mile of scree slope, as I'd done a dozen times before, to go and locate my ball. I didn't have the wherewithal to keep going. I was a failure, and Zinadine—had he been there—would have laughed. I admitted defeat.

Of course, I caught up with Bob a half-hour later and we continued on for the next few days, camping in La Niña's bountiful rains and even climbing Capitol Peak en route to the trailhead, enjoying one of the finest wilderness treks I've ever experienced. We returned totally happy, safe, and I really felt as though we'd experienced the area we live in the way it should be experienced, not just as a pretty view that the typical vacationer gets from his Aspen condo or as a view from a bus window that downvalley workers get as they're transported upvalley to resort jobs.

As for the dribbling challenge, it remains to be met. The 15-odd miles of rugged terrain could easily be dribbled, but the successful party will have to show fortitude, cunning, and even a bit of daring to get through the rock bands at the head of Avalanche Creek. It remains a challenge for future mountaineers, future World Cup players, future knuckleheads with a lot of time on their hands. And when they come and seek my advice, I'll advise a lobotomy. It requires a big sharp point.

Out of the Box in Hong Kong

(Hong Kong, 2000)

"Reinforced concrete has brought about a revolution in the aesthetics of construction."
—Le Corbusier (Charles-Édouard Jeanneret), *Towards a New Architecture*

A couple of years ago, if you'd asked me where Hong Kong was and what it was like, I would've guessed, "big city in Asia." The most I knew about the place was Jackie Chan, Jackie Chan and Jackie Chan. Pretty lame for a well-traveled adventurer.

The opportunity to alter my understanding of the place arose in late 2000, when a travel-writing junket came my way in December. While I was inquiring about visas, Diana Budiman of the Hong Kong Tourist Association told me if I really liked outdoor activities as I claimed, that I'd really enjoy Hong Kong.

Adventure activities? Outdoors? Seriously? She had to be kidding.

Ever since Hong Kong was first created and inhabited (which must be several thousand years ago), there has likely been no more than a few dozen articles and maybe a handful of books written about its outdoors. The city is better known as a glittering, fast-paced commercial hub—Las Vegas meets Rodeo Drive or Times Square on steroids. But this city-state of seven million has two completely different faces: the dense, adrenaline-filled rush of pure urbanity; and the quiet, lush, and totally compelling outdoors. Hong Kong, if you will, is really two places. The human and the non-human. The boxes—as I like to call the built environment—and the bush.

During a long Cathay Pacific flight that circled around the northern perimeter of the Pacific Ocean and nearly left the earth's gravitational field, I read a few recent news clippings about Hong Kong. During the latter 20th century Hong Kong was in the news quite a bit because the colony was handed back to China after more than 150 years under British rule. Before the 1997 handover occurred, political analysts, journalists and much of the general public expected the proposed Sino-British Joint Declaration (which called for the Chinese government to employ a hands-off approach to ruling Hong Kong) to be nothing more than lip service. It was feared the people of Hong Kong were about to be muzzled, both socially and politically. Some businesses relocated to Singapore and other Pacific Rim cities, many Westerners moved out, and East Asia prepared for a jolt.

Of course, after a round of fireworks over Victoria Harbour on June 30, 1997, and some tearful speeches by Chris Patten, Hong Kong's last British governor, the expectations fueled by Tiannemen Square and the Chinese-Tibetan situation fizzled. The dire predictions about the Chinese rule did not come true and, from a historical perspective, were probably questionable to begin with. "Some of the worst fears about heavy-handed Chinese rule over Hong Kong have so far not come to pass," reported *The New York Times* [on Jan. 17 2001]. "Just last weekend some 1,200 members of the Falun Gong sect (a group that practices a form of exercise, similar to Tai Chi), which has been heavily persecuted on the mainland, were allowed to hold a mass gathering in a concert hall owned by the Hong Kong government."

The British handover coincided loosely with the Asian financial crisis of the late 1990s. The day after Hong Kong went back under Chinese rule, Thailand devalued its currency, the bhat, causing—in part—the entire Eastern Hemisphere to grind into an economic slump. Hong Kong made headlines again, but mostly because it is the Western financial center for the Eastern world and its economy—like Tokyo's—was an icon of Asian prosperity. Hong Kong has never made headlines because of its outdoor activities. For the past 30 years, the city has been famous as Asia's top industrial trade hub and for its dynamic, fast-paced retail life, and for its great martial arts movies. People think of electronics, clothes, shoes and jewelry when the topic of Hong Kong comes up; not trail running, rock climbing and sea kayaking.

Luckily, for me, I hadn't seen back-in-the-good-old-days Hong Kong, before the Chinese takeover, and I wasn't a connoisseur of the art of shopping. I'd seen a photo of someone rock climbing on Kowloon Peak, and that's I wanted to do—go rock climbing.

Ironically, when I started at the University of Colorado as an undergraduate in 1983, the first book I ever encountered in Norlin Library's Rare Books collection, was a rock climbing guide to Hong Kong (called, predictably enough, *Rock Climbs of Hong Kong*). If memory serves, it was a book dated to the mid-1950s. My closest companion of the period, Benny Bach, and I used to break up our long hours in the library with trips into Rare Books to examine and ponder this gem. Of course, the ancient pages of the tome couldn't handle much in the way of enthusiastic fondling, so after about three nights it was in tatters and we had to content ourselves with other rare books (like *An Historical Guide to Boulder County Irrigation Ditches: Vol IX*) lest studying get in the way of a pleasant evening out. *Rock Climbs of Hong Kong*? Was the author serious? Who knew?

The plane banked into its final turn and we came rumbling down onto the runway. Out my window I could just make out the city's form: stacked vertical columns lit up like blockish Christmas trees spread across shimmering water. This looked like a fine city.

I caught a taxi into town and found my way to the Salisbury YMCA in the wonderfully named Tsim Sha Tsui, an area of Kowloon, the peninsula jutting into Victoria Harbour from the north.

The Salisbury YMCA isn't really a YMCA—rather, it's a really posh hotel. I was shown to a room on the 12th floor, which although small, was well-appointed with a stocked fridge, two single, neatly made beds and a desk with a comfortable chair. Everything was slightly smaller, slightly daintier than you'd find in an equivalent hotel in the States, but incredibly clean, neat and appealing. Young Christian men in Asia must be regarded highly.

I dumped my bags, made a cup of tea (one of the benefits of visiting former British colonies) and headed out into the streets to find my old pal Benny. Benny, never one to miss an interesting place, had flown in two days prior and was in a hotel just down the street. When I'd mentioned I was going to Hong Kong, Benny and his girlfriend, Angie Moquin, had traded in some frequent-flier miles and decided to join me. I descended to Hankow Road, then wandered up to Peking Road, turned right toward Nathan Road, and was pleasantly surprised to find myself looking at the infamous Chungking Mansions. Chungking Mansions is not what it might sound like (I don't know about you, but to me the name conjures up a villa in the French countryside serving Chinese food.)

Chungking Mansions is actually a rotten old concrete structure known for being something of a small city unto itself. Inside are dozens of small hotels, some occupying a few rooms on each floor, some occupying whole floors. These hotels have names like Imperial Gardens Hotel and Chungking Boarding House, but the names do little to describe the physical form these hotels take. They are, simply, a collection of starkly lit, filthy box-shaped rooms with cheap cruddy furniture, and generally very little in the way of windows or other access to air. One guidebook to Hong Kong calls Chungking Mansions "a high-rise dump," which sums it up rather accurately. I glanced back toward the Salisbury YMCA and thought of my government-paid-for room, and smiled.

Benny was, of course, holed up in a building next door to the Chungking Mansions, which turned out to be the unofficial twin brother of the Chungking Mansions. He met me on the street then led me up a tight stairway to a narrow hall with dozens of seedy-looking people going in all directions. He mentioned the name of the hotel as we squeezed past several young men in the hall—I could have sworn he said "Fire Hazard." We turned a corner, and Benny opened a door.

Benny's room must have been about eight-by-ten feet, and about eight feet high. Its walls were completely finished with white bathroom tiles—"so you can hose it down," Benny suggested. A large fluorescent light buzzed overhead. It reminded me of looking in the fridge at midnight. The entire room was filled with two large, rickety wooden beds that seemed bigger than the available space. How they were carried up the stairs and squeezed into such a small, confined space was an intriguing mystery until it was suggested they were built in-situ.

Angie was lying on one of the beds studying a book about Hong Kong. She looked up when we arrived, her face a mixture of desperation and sadness. (This is why I like traveling with Benny—he might be able to afford $80 a night for a decent hotel room, such as found at the Salisbury YMCA—but cheap rooms, like his digs at the Kowloon Fire Hazard Inn, offer infinite challenge and adventure, the likes of which most tourists will never experience.)

Benny interrupted my thoughts by pointing out the "bathroom." The bathroom (and I use the term loosely here) was a square space about the size of an old phone booth. It was built into one wall, and a toilet sat in its center. Attached to the wall on the left side of the toilet was a sink—it was one of those arrangements where you can put your elbow on the sink, prop your head up in your palm and have a very pensive and leisurely crap. Above the toilet was, of course, a showerhead.

"Looks like you could be on the can, shave and shower all at the same time," I suggested.

"Yeah, and check this out," Benny said. One of the giant beds was crammed up so hard against the "bathroom" that you could stand on it, while peeing into the toilet. Benny did me the favor of demonstrating the stance but not the arc. I thought of my beloved Salisbury YMCA and felt warm and fuzzy.

We went out into the streets and wandered around for as long as possible before Benny and Angie eventually returned to the Kowloon Fire Hazard Inn and I to the Salisbury YMCA. The following morning they moved in with me.

Once Benny and Angie were comfortably ensconced in the extra bed in Room 1202 of the Salisbury YMCA, we gathered gear together and headed for the Tsim Sha Tsui MTR (Mass Transit Railway) station and worked our way onto a train for Central, the downtown part of Hong Kong. Not once, in 20 years of climbing, have I taken a bus or subway for a mountain experience, but as I quickly learned, Hong Kong is unique in every aspect—including its outdoors. At Central we switched trains and rode the subway out to Chai Wan, on the eastern side of Victoria Island. There, we caught a European-style double-decker bus and headed for a beach town called Shek-O, which is surrounded by brown granite domes popping up out of the water. The rock climbing at Shek-O, we soon learned, is superb. The orange-brown granite crags of Shek-O are some of best I've ever touched. The rock is coarse but compact, just like California's Joshua Tree or Wyoming's Vedauwoo climbing areas.

Sea cliff climbing is rare in the Americas; decent ocean-side cliffs simply don't exist. It is a much more European tradition, especially for the British, whose small but varied island is rimmed by a very three-dimensional coast. Since Hong Kong has been British for so long, and it's geographically similar to the Mother Isle in terms of its rocky coast, it's no surprise that the coastline cliffs have been well developed for climbing. Many of the best crags are over the water, making for atmospheric and inspiring climbing.

Of course, after our day at Shek-O, it rained for two days. Benny, Angie and I had to be content with wandering around the city in a downpour while thumbing through the sodden pages of the 1994 edition of *Rock Climbs of Hong Kong*, bumming out that we were wasting so much time. Benny and Angie flew home a few days later, just when the weather was drying up, so I arranged to do things with Hong Kong locals with whom I'd been put in touch by the Hong Kong Tourist Association.

Over the remainder of my visit, I got to sea kayak for many miles through the clear blue waters around the Sai Kung Peninsula with local kayak guide Paul Etherington; climb at several crags, including the 600-foot tall cliffs on Kowloon Peak with Paul's brother in-law Guy Bigwood and his girlfriend Janet Cheung; and trail-run on Lantau Island's 3,000-foot Phoenix Peak (popular with peak-baggers). These are parts of Hong Kong most people—except a few diehard Westerners—don't ever see, or even have the desire to see. From my perspective, they are missing the best part of this strange little Chinese sub-nation. I've never been so impressed with a major city's great outdoors. Why would anyone want to squander time in Chungking Mansions or the Kowloon Fire Hazard Inn when there's so much to do outside?

To understand Hong Kong's vast outdoors, the city and its physical surroundings first need a little explanation. Hong Kong is not just one big city, perched on the edge of Asia against the South China Sea. Hong Kong is, for all intents and purposes, a small, geographically diverse nation (the Hong Kong Special Administrative Region or SAR). This nation occupies a peninsula attached to mainland China, as well as an archipelago of some 235 islands of various sizes scattered around the peninsula. The total land area is 1,070 square kilometers. The city part of Hong Kong—the part you already know about—lies mostly on two sides of a small harbor, Victoria Harbour, on the southern edge of the archipelago.

More important than the physical layout of Hong Kong is the manner in which the built environment has evolved, or rather, not evolved. In Hong Kong, there are no suburbs. The built up parts of Hong Kong are as built up as any place on earth, with skyscrapers up to 50, 60, 70 stories and more. Meanwhile, you can step across a street and literally be in temperate jungle wilderness. There are no Western American-style 35-acre ranchettes or sprawling subdivisions cluttering up the surface of the earth. It's all huge buildings (of little boxes) or wilderness. Even Hong Kong Island, a 78-square-kilometer island where downtown is located, is mostly natural land.

According to government figures, about 40 percent of Hong Kong's entire land area is formally set aside for conservation in 23 Country and Marine parks. Most of the rest of the land area of the Hong Kong SAR remains undeveloped, too, and having seen a lot of it from many angles, I would venture to guess as much as 75 percent of the land remains in a natural state.

Hong Kong's outdoors are so impressive that by the fourth chapter of Damian Harper and Robert Storey's Lonely Planet guide to Hong Kong, they're talking about the region's wilds: "Hong Kong has surprising natural retreats for lovers of the big outdoors. A short ferry ride away is Lamma Island, an overgrown idyll that nature enthusiasts will find hard to resist," they wrote. "The New Territories cuts a huge swath to the North, offering bracing walks among dramatic and spectacular countryside."

Biologically, Hong Kong is more diverse than all the Western United States combined. Until almost a decade ago, Hong Kong's native flora and fauna was little documented. Then, in the early 1990s, the World Wide Fund for Nature helped fund a study that among other things revealed 210 types of seaweed, 175 types of fern, 1,900 flowering plants (including 120 orchid species), 2,000 moth species, 225 butterflies, 107 dragonflies, 96 freshwater fish species, 23 amphibians, 78 reptiles, 445 birds, and 57 mammals (including civets and macaques). Not bad for a place regarded as Asia's biggest shopping mall.

Despite all this great outdoorsy stuff which I enjoyed immensely, Hong Kong is not famous for its rock climbing, sea kayaking and trail running. It is famous for Jackie Chan and knockoffs. Jackie Chan is an actor whose films have become phenomenally popular worldwide and who, hopefully, needs no introduction. Jackie Chan is my hero. He'll be your hero too, once you see one of his films. (I recently did a web search and found over a quarter million web pages mentioning Jackie Chan—that's how cool he is.) It's no wonder that he's become a marketing tool for the Hong Kong government.

Meanwhile, knock-offs are brand name clothes and shoes that have been manufactured without consent of the brand owner. In other words, just as there are millions of Jackie Chan videos circling the globe, there are also millions of articles of fake clothing, shoes and accessories illegally labeled Nike, Adidas, Ralph Lauren, Tommy Hilfiger, Rolex, Coach, Louis Vuitton, The Gap, Eddie Bauer, WalMart, and J.C. Penney.

The knock-off business is a worldwide game. In 1982, it was estimated that the illegal knock-off business cost the U.S. economy $5.5 billion in lost jobs and profits as well as in law enforcement expenses. The estimate was revised in 1998 to $66 billion, and then to $200 billion in 1999. What it costs the entire world is a number I haven't found. But it's Hong Kong that has been at the center of the knockoff industry for many years, not because counterfeit products are necessarily made in the City of Life but because Hong Kong is a major business hub for the region.

Sitting close to mainland China, Taiwan, Vietnam, Thailand and other poor Southeast Asian nations where the stuff is made, Hong Kong is a town filled with agents, business managers and manufacturing sub-contractors of big name footwear and clothing apparel. Most are conducting legitimate trade, and are overseeing the manufacturing of their goods. But others are doing less than honorable work, organizing the manufacture and shipping of questionable products with million-dollar labels on them.

And still others are spies. The clothing, footwear and accessories industries are so big they have their own spies working diligently to catch and prosecute counterfeiters. They roam the backalleys, factories and ports of Southeast Asia looking for fake shoes, clothes, purses, and belts. The counterfeit industry is so big in Southeast Asia that dozens of law firms from around the globe have branches there dealing—in many cases—primarily with knockoffs.

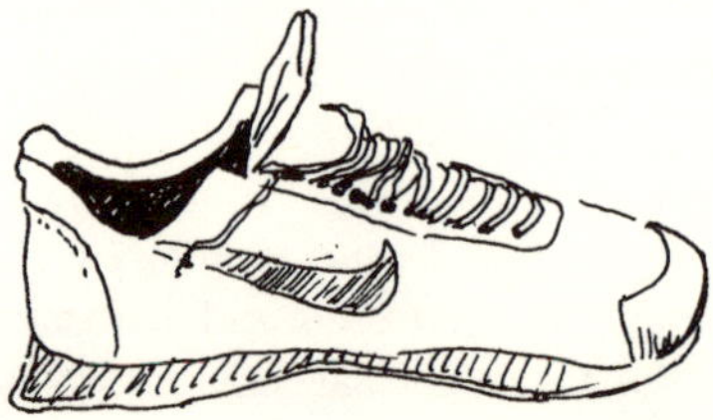

One law firm in Bangkok, Tilleke & Gibbins, has done so much work with knockoff goods that they've actually created a museum dedicated to these artifacts. And this is an amazing thing. I'll quote from Tilleke & Gibbins excellent web page: "The Tilleke & Gibbins Museum of Counterfeit Goods was established in 1989 at the firm's Bangkok, Thailand office. However, long before that time, the firm had already in hand the main prerequisites to start a museum in the form of a large volume of counterfeit and pirated goods accumulated over the years from raids conducted on behalf of the firm's clients. The goods, which were used as evidence in court, were then stashed away in boxes, taking up valuable storage space and serving no purpose whatsoever. With the collection growing rapidly, it became apparent that a way should be found which would take advantage of the counterfeit goods and turn them from the liability they were posing to a useful purpose."

Tilleke & Gibbins's then senior partner David Lyman realized that his firm's collection of ripped off stuff might "prove useful as educational tools if properly displayed and accessible for public viewing" and a museum was born. The museum started out with about 100 items separated into several areas: clothing, leather goods, electronics and toiletries. "However, with new items gathered on a continuing basis from raids overseen by the firm, plus samples of the genuine goods which the firm obtains, the collection has rapidly grown. At present, the museum has approximately 1500 pieces of infringing trademark and copyrighted goods, making it the largest one of its kind in Thailand."

From a quick look at the museum (visible online at www.tginfo.com/museum/museum.htm) it's clear that Tilleke & Gibbins's lawyers aren't messing around. If you look in the section called "Edible Products" there is a picture of a box of Mrs. Fields Cookies. Sitting next to it is a similar box with a very similar design, except the words say *Denis' Cookies*, not Mrs. Fields Cookies. To the left and below the cookie infraction are two bars of chocolate. The upper one is a bar of our good old friend Toblerone, that great Swiss stuff that breaks off in the triangular chunks and is the single best gift to have on hand when disembarking a plane from Europe. Below the bar of Toblerone is a similarly shaped bar of something called *Tamborine*.

"These counterfeit packagings of edible products (left) differ only slightly from the genuine packagings (right)," states the photo caption. "At a glance, many non-regular consumers would mistake the counterfeit version for the original. As for the goods themselves, one can never tell if they meet health and safety standards."

As I said, these lawyers aren't messing around. Obviously, there has been an infraction of some kind of copyrighted packaging and name recognition thing—Denis and the folks at Tamborine Chocolate Co. have trodden on sacred ground. But let's look at the bigger picture. Who doesn't love traveling to foreign lands and seeing stuff like bars of Tamborine Chocolate and Denis' Cookies? I mean, sure, they're ripping off the designs and the names, but these lawyers seem to fail to realize the entertainment value here is greater than any missed cookie or chocolate bar sales. Who hasn't giggled at an Adigas T-shirt on a poor Mexican farmer, or chuckled with glee over a L.A. Lackers jersey in the African countryside? I've had the opportunity to do both, and found the experiences intensely rewarding.

Heck, I've never bought Mrs. Fields Cookies, but I sure would buy myself a box of Denis' Cookies if the opportunity arose *simply because they are Denis' Cookies.* (Perhaps Mrs. Fields would be wise to rip off Denis and start calling her product Mrs. Denis Fields Cookies, but I digress ...)

The night after climbing at Shek-O, Benny, Angie and I wandered the Temple Street night market for many hours (even my Salisbury YMCA room, we decided, was cramped). Here, in block after block of closed-off streets filled with stalls and vendors and all sorts of bright lights, it's possible to buy anything. I bought silk shirts, underwear and robes, all with interesting names and logos. The underwear had "Rock Star" on the label, the shirts were made by a company that put no label in the product, and the robes had a Chinese character. The 20 silk ties I purchased all had South Park and Warner Bros. characters on them, undoubtedly sans permission from the owners of the images. The best was a vest with the label Versanni, which I can only imagine was meant to be a Versace knockoff. Heck, who can fault the Chinese factory workers making the stuff. Versanni, Versace, it must all read the same to them. Ironically, four months after I had wandered down from rock climbing on Kowloon Peak through the Tung Choi Street neighborhood in Hong Kong's Mong Kok neighborhood, customs officers seized $1.3 million worth of counterfeit goods.

"In the first case, Customs officers of Trade Descriptions Investigation Division in an anti-counterfeiting operation, seized about 4,300 pieces of garment and 1,300 counterfeit leather goods," said a news statement. "In another case, Customs officers at Lok Ma Chau Control Point seized 9,802 pairs of shoes, all bearing false origin labels, worth about $1.06 million,

from an incoming lorry. Among the seizure, 810 pairs were counterfeit shoes."

So what happens to counterfeit goods? When knockoff artists are busted, often the company they work for and the local police insist on destroying the goods, usually by burning them. In early 2000, the athletic shoe company New Balance helped police nab counterfeiters in Indonesia, who had manufactured some 160,000 pairs of knockoff shoes.

"The shoes, called New Basket, Dallas Star, and One Star, which infringed upon both New Balance and Converse trademarks, were burned publicly at the police headquarters in West Java," stated a May 9, 2000, New Balance press release. "This event represented the largest seizure/destruction of counterfeit footwear in Asia to date."

Certainly, the knockoff trade is a truly massive industry. But you've got to wonder whether destroying all these counterfeit shoes is such a great idea. Aren't they still wearable, regardless of the label on the side? The amount of resources gobbled up when 160,000 pairs of shoes are burned must be huge. Certainly the carbon emissions generated through the destruction of these illegal goods must be sizeable, and the resources and energy required to re-manufacture 160,000 pairs of shoes can't be cheap either.

One has to wonder whether New Balance's marketing plan wouldn't have been better aided if the company (and law-enforcement officials) had simply seized the shoes, then sent them to charities.

John Larsen, New Balance's president emeritus at the time commented in a press release, "New Balance has a worldwide campaign against counterfeiting. Counterfeiting robs trademark owners of the revenue they are entitled to. Furthermore, consumers who buy fraudulent products don't get the warranties, service, and quality that New Balance guarantees."

New Balance Athletic Shoe, Inc. employs more than 2,000 people around the globe, and in 1999 reported worldwide sales of $890 million. Who knows: if 160,000 pairs of knocked off athletic shoes were donated to poor knockoff shoemakers they might take up running, or at least walking. They might then realize that burning counterfeit shoes hurts their lungs and they might try to find work doing something less environmentally destructive. Probably not, but you never know. At least the shoes might get them out of their depressing high-rise boxes like the Kowloon Fire Hazard Inn for a few hours.

What I—a Western U.S. resident and enthusiastic outdoor adventure type—find strange is that the local Chinese residents seem to have little interest in any outdoor activities. When I went hiking on the peaks above the Choi Hung neighborhood, I had the place to myself. Rock climbing—on any of Hong Kong's cliffs—there's no one around; sea kayaking for two full days around Sai Kung, Paul and I saw a few fishermen but certainly no other kayakers; trail running on Lantau it was just the birds and I.

The Japanese and Koreans are nutty about skiing and running and climbing. Japan boasts the biggest indoor ski slopes on earth, and last time I was big-walling on El Capitan in Yosemite Valley, there were several Korean teams slaving away. But the Chinese of Hong Kong seem uninterested. Taiwan, I was told, is similar. A large island covered with some of Asia's most beautiful outdoors, it boasts great hiking, climbing, camping, kayaking … whatever you like. There, I know of a man—a friend of a friend—who owns an outdoor equipment shop. He has no competition, yet sales are so small he has trouble staying in business.

That's not to say Southeastern Asia's people are backward or uninspired—to the contrary. I found Hong Kong's Chinese some of the most polite, considerate, hard-working and orderly folks on earth. In fact, they are—in almost every way—far in advance of us Westerners. Their streets are spotless, their society is immaculately ordered and their technological innovations seem constantly ahead.

So, maybe that's what makes Hong Kong so unique. The built, human, urban side of Hong Kong is amazing—outdistancing most Western urban areas in terms of civility and functionality by leaps and bounds. Yet, on the other hand, Hong Kong's pristine, rugged, untrammeled outdoors is among some of the finest anywhere. It's a combination that's hard to fathom, yet easy to experience. Step off a subway and within a few steps you can be hiking; hop out a taxi door and you can be next to a seriously good cragging cliff; get off the bus and across the street you squeeze into a sea kayak. It's a great mix, easily worth shaking up your senses and every preconceived notion you've ever had about Hong Kong. After all, Hong Kong is really two places. The human and the non-human.

In Hong Kong there's life inside the box, so to speak, and life out of the box. I liked both.

Round about Wales

(Wales, 2001)

"It's not unusual for girls to throw their underwear at Welsh crooner Tom Jones,"
—Lonely Planet, *Britain*

Wales. Mention the name and most Americans think you're going to an aquarium-based themepark, to some kind of new discount superstore, or worse—a sporting event where the team mascot is a large deep-sea mammal ("A Whales game? Who are the Whales?" I was asked by one eager sports fan. "They that new franchise in Fort Lauderdale?")

When you explain it's a small nation in Britain, wedged between England and the Irish Sea, blank stares tend to come flying at you faster than incomplete orders at your local fast-food restaurant drive-through.

I don't mind. I like Wales. I'm sort of glad no one knows about it. In early 2001, I was invited to help some of my co-workers on a consulting job in Hereford, in Western England. The consulting gig (I was to help write a report) was to last four days. After that, my wife Ann and I decided we'd take a weeklong auto tour of Southern Wales. We had just had Zoe, our first child (well, Ann had had our first child—I hung around nervously and tried to be a contributing member of the hospital staff), and we thought that a trip to Wales might be a good introduction to traveling with small children, a sort of weird experimental parental challenge—like thumb screws or the rack.

Wales has always fascinated me. Tucked up in the crook of England's belly, it's wholly overshadowed by England's bigger and better understood neighbors, Scotland and Ireland. Most tourists don't do Wales. It seems most people who visit this nation of nearly three million are Londoners going hillwalking in Snowdonia. The remainder seems to be tourists of various nationalities heading for Scotland who get lost on West England byways and end up vacuumed away by confusing road signs to places like Llanfihangel Crucorney or Llanthony or Llandrindod Wells or Llanfihangel-Nant-Melan or or Llansantffrad-ym-Mechain, probably wondering if their inflight drugs are still in effect.

The correct pronunciation of these places is one of the great mysteries of the British Isles, a mystery on par with who built Stonehenge. As I drove west, out of Hereford, I soon learned they are completely and undeniably unpronounceable, except by Welshmen, who are likewise incomprehensible.

"Ann, you need to navigate since I'll be driving on the left and it's been a while. Okay?"

"Okay, Cam. Turn onto the road to Laannnfinnagelcruckorny."

"To what?"

"Laannnfinnagelcruckorny."

"How do you spell it?"

"Double ll-a-n-f-i-h-"

As we spun through several million rotations of the first of several million roundabouts we were about to experience, I attempted to lean over and look at the map. There it was, as Ann spelled it, Llanfihangel Crucorney. Plain as could be. It appeared to not be entirely in Wales, sort of on the border, but the name was enough to make me circle eight more times around the roundabout until I was absolutely sure we were headed in that direction.

"Hey, you're headed back to Hereford!" Ann announced.

"Am I?"

"Aren't we supposed to go to Brecon?"

"Aren't we?"

A long silenced followed as we watched the road. It appeared we were headed somewhere, but exactly where was something of a mystery. Then, all of a sudden, as is common on British roads, a sign flew past stating "Wormbridge: 2" or something to that effect.

"We're definitely headed back toward Hereford," Ann suggested.

"Well, Wormbridge sounds okay," I added, gazing at the sky in an effort to divine north and south.

This is what kills me when it comes to driving in Britain: there are no major landforms with which to guide oneself. In the western United States where I live, there are generally mountain ranges that run some direction, and are easy to follow. The Front Range in Colorado, for example, lets you know where north and south are. In Britain, even the sky—where the sun normally resides and is a good indicator of south and north—is generally of little use. Here, you have a great gray smear overhead—about as useful as a watercolor highway map that's been soaking in the Thames.

I slowed down and found an appropriate place to redirect our expedition and we continued on our way.

"Laannnfinnagelcruckorny here we come!" I said, triumphantly. While I'm sure Llanfihangel Crucorney is a lovely place, the target of our day's travel was Brecon (a.k.a. "Aberhonddu"), and we proceeded past Llanfihangel Crucorney down to a place called Abergavenny before we found the roundabout that would siphon us off onto the Aberhonddu road. When we finally did make it to Aberhonddu (a.k.a. Brecon) I was exhausted. Driving on the left, which I hadn't done for 13 years, was like frying eggs using a sheet of foil in your hands—all balance and stress.

At least Brecon provided some respite. Brecon is cool. I like Brecon a lot. I can pronounce Brecon. Brecon is—from what I read later—considered one of the five prettiest villages in Wales (the others are Betws-y-Coed, Llanberis, St. Davids, and Dolgellau). Perched on the edge of the Brecon Beacons National Park (essentially an area of high hills), it leans out over the Welsh countryside like a decrepit old man, assuring the community that there's something greater in the land than the nearby humanity. (This is what London needs really badly.)

We took a room at the George Hotel and began exploring town. Brecon is situated on the slope of a hill at the juncture of several streams, and it's this semi-vertical aspect of the town that makes it so picturesque. Ann, Zoe and I wandered along all the town's streets amazed at the commerce and social interaction. There were no Wal-Marts, Kmarts or McDonalds (that we found), or edge-of-town malls to displace the healthy vibrant community. The only downer was the smoke from burning carcasses—Wales was in the midst of the 2001 Foot and Mouth disaster. The smell and smoke from burning animals was everywhere.

On the hillside above town, we found the Brecon Cathedral, a stunning chunk of history with a beautiful garden surrounding it. In the garden, we met a few crazies—no kidding. From what we were able to gather, the five men in this group were incredibly simple, a couple of whom seemed to be recovering town drunks. They were, apparently, rebuilding a five-century-old garden, and although we spent roughly two hours talking with these charming chaps about the garden, about all we were able to ascertain about the project was that they were, apparently, rebuilding a five century-old garden.

One of the non-verbal things I noticed about the guys digging in the Brecon Cathedral grounds was that they all looked a bit like me. Since you have no idea what I look like, I'll describe briefly: a huge pumpkin head with a hooked, broken nose and giant tufts of wiry gray hair sticking out of my ears and nose. Of mostly Scots-Irish descent, a fair amount of Welsh blood has been drizzled into the recipe so the similarity might not have been coincidental. I might have been looking at long-lost cousins and uncles. And—my wife pointed out in regards to the crazy gibberish being spoken—perhaps my future.

After Zoe had had a short meltdown (a load of poop, followed by loud wailing and a refusal of the bottle, then a refusal of the breast, followed by more poop and more wailing), we meandered back to the George Hotel, dined on Welsh lamb and slept like rocks. In the morning, we headed south and west, towards the Gower Peninsula.

In Wales, and all of Britain really, a major challenge to the non-British motoring public is the simple fact that the road signs aren't very comprehensible, and this became apparent as we motored south toward the Gower Peninsula. Slowing down before one intersection, I saw there were small square signs on both sides of the road with slashes on them. Initial three-slash signs were followed 100 yards later by two-slash signs, which were followed 100 yards later by one-slash signs.

If these slash signs were some kind of universal symbol for "slow down to three because you're coming upon an intersection, then slow down to two, and now slow down to one," it wasn't readily apparent. The small square signs might as well have said "giant radioactive earthworms in this area: watch out," for all we knew. I had to wonder what non-English speakers thought. Certainly I couldn't find three, two and one slashes marked around the speedometer.

Confusing signs were most abundant near roundabouts, just when you really want to be confused. It took Ann (our navigator) about five days to notice and realize that there were several signs, each with distinct purposes, preceding every roundabout. The first was usually a large green sign with white lettering showing Britain's premier circular fantasy. The major destinations, which could be accessed from it, were clearly labeled. Then there was a second sign, slightly smaller, with black writing on a white background. This second sign depicted local destinations, often without road numbers. However, sometimes these secondary signs did include road numbers, if, as I was told later by an English acquaintance who explained in these exact words, "the local destinations were along A or B roads, but C roads have no numbers, unlike France, which has it sussed."

Hmm ...

Of course, whether you're driving on an A, B, C, D, E or F road is really what matters in Britain. A roads are major thoroughfares, where the number of signs matches the volume of the traffic. B roads are less in volume, fewer in signs. On C roads you're lucky to find a sign at all. The rest, you're lucky to find the road.

The Gower Peninsula did not offer less difficult motoring—actually, it became trickier. As we traversed this thumb of land sticking out the bottom of Wales like a misplaced appendix, we slowly learned that there were no hotels anywhere on the entire peninsula with rooms available.

"Bunk 'Ollodai Weekind," we were informed by a tavern keeper.

The Gower (*Penrhyn Gwyr* in Welsh, if you like) is a bastion of Welsh summer resorts, so the fact there was a holiday was a double whammy. Especially the dreaded Bunk 'Ollodai.

The British Bank Holiday is similar to America's Memorial Day. It's when hordes of winter-weary suburbanites cram into their cars, get out on the highways, and switch off their brains. After nearly killing one another with their autos, they turn their attention toward filling up all the hotels in the land, including bed-and-breakfasts and campgrounds. If they survive, this is followed by other activities, like driving home.

Ann, Zoe and I scoured the Gower Peninsula, from the popular seaside resort called The Mumbles ("My mother belongs here!" Ann said, astonished that we had discovered such a place) to Wormshead, a stunning and poorly named chunk of earth sticking out over the Irish Sea.

We drove the byways and highways of Gower, stopping at every B&B and every hotel—all were full. We finally found a B&B in an old schoolhouse near Oxwich Bay. The room was decorated like a dollhouse, with dozens of doilies and armies of porcelain figures cramming up all available space. But at least it was a bed. I swept 500 porcelain people, farm animals, and characters from children's books off the nightstand and dumped my bag on the top. It was good to unwind.

The next day we headed north and west to Fishguard. Fishguard wasn't really where we wanted to go. However, it was still Bunk 'Ollodai Weekind, and the only hotel I could find for miles around that had any space was the Fishguard Bay Hotel.

Fishguard was at the limit of our driving day. Ann and I had been trying to restrict our driving time each day to under four hours, for Zoe's sake (which was, in turn, for our sake), but the several hours spent twisting through roundabouts each day was blowing our time budget. Fishguard, it turned out, was a four-hour drive away with minimal roundabouts. And, it was a nice little town, too.

British ferry towns, of which Fishguard is one, have a reputation for being untidy, unsophisticated little places—the kinds of towns people run through quickly en route to a bouncing ferry to Ireland. To the contrary, Fishguard was quaint. It was friendly, it was picturesque, it was neat. Too bad Fishguard sounds like some form of feminine protection or a metal grate that goes over an irrigation ditch.

And the Fishguard Bay Hotel—wow! An historic building of a half dozen floors overlooking the bay, with a lounge, bar, two restaurants and a fabulously friendly staff. We got a huge room with a separate bathroom and a balcony overlooking the bay for only £70. I felt like a 1940s movie star or character from a spy novel. ("Ann, you distract Zoe while I go meet Rachivinsky at the docks and eat the microfilm!") With the Bunk 'Ollodai milieu taking place all around, we stayed two nights.

Pronouncing Welsh isn't that bad. The worst thing was the double L, and it was names like Llanfihangel, Llanthony, Llandrindod and Llansantffrad that were tripping us up—you know, the easy ones. So I tried to remember how I'd learned to pronounce them as a kid. In 1976, I'd had the opportunity to visit Wales with my parents and sisters, and it was during that visit that my father had figured out how to pronounce double L in Welsh: "thl."

We'd spent a good deal of time in Dolgellau during that 1976 trip mastering practicing our "thls," and likely had it mastered, but 25 years is a long time. As happens with all of my father's language conquests (and "thl" was a pretty big conquest), they tend to slide back toward a more casual pronunciation. So between 1976 and this year, Dolgethlie had morphed ever so slowly into *Dolgelly*. ("Remember when we went to Dolgelly, son?")

Visiting Wales now, I was curious to see if Dad's 1976 pronunciation was still accurate. Or whether the pronunciation had changed, as—I hoped—Welsh people had learned what Anglo-Saxon, Teutonic and Latin consonants are supposed to sound like.

Whenever I want truth and accuracy, I go online, as I did shortly before our trip. I found 6,000 web pages matching "Welsh language."

One web page stated: "Ll—roughly pronounced 'thl,' eg: Llanberis (thlan-berris)." Another web page stated: "Pronounced like an s but from the sides of the tongue rather than the front." A third offered this useful tidbit: "Ll is an aspirated l. That means you form your lips and tongue to pronounce l, but then you blow air gently around the sides of the tongue instead of saying anything. Got it? The nearest you can get to this sound in English is to pronounce it as an l with a th in front of it. Welsh words: llan (thlan); llawr (thlour); llwyd (thlooid)." Finally, yet another web page told me, "Ll is not found in English, but is very common in Welsh. Put your tongue in position as though you were going to make an 'l' sound, but blow out instead."

Sure, just blow out instead—piece of cake. I was just damn happy we weren't headed to Llanfairpwllgwyngyllgogerychwyrndrobwllllantysiliogogogoch, a town in North Wales known for selling souvenir T-shirts as wide as circus tents (the only size big enough to hold all the letters) and gift mugs that hold 80 gallons (again, the only size big enough to hold all the letters).

This curious town was originally named Llanfair Pwllgwyngyll, which translates as The-Mary-church-by-the-pool-near-the-white-hazels. However, a train was built from Chester to Holyhead in the mid-19th century, and local marketeers wanted a better way to unload circus-tent-sized T-shirts and 80-gallon mugs. At the suggestion of a local cobbler, the village was renamed Llanfairpwllgwyngyllgogerychwyrndrobwllllantysiliogogogoch, which means St.-Mary's-church-in-the-hollow-of-the-white-hazel-near-a-rapid-whirlpool-and-the-church-of-St.-Tysilio-of-the-red-cave. (By the way, I just read that llanfairpwllgwyngyllgogerychwyrndrobwllllantysiliogogogoch.com is the longest domain name registered in the world—and people say the Welsh aren't doing anything noteworthy.)

I honestly think Llanfairpwllgwyngyllgogerychwyrndrobwllllantysiliogogogoch should change its name again. After all, why settle for merely being St.-Mary's-church-in-the-hollow-of-the-white-hazel-near-a-rapid-whirlpool-and-the-church-of-St.-Tysilio-of-the-red-cave when you could be St.-Mary's-church-in-the-hollow-of-the-white-hazel-near-a-rapid-whirlpool-and-the-church-of-St.-Tysilio-of-the-red-cave-in-the-north-of-Wales-near-the-Sea-of-Irish-and-the-waves-of-ocean-with-the-English-nearby-designing-confusing-roundabouts-and-incomprehensible-road-signs? It was just a thought.

After two days down south, Ann, Zoe and I headed north. Our trip was specifically South Wales, as we had only five or six days. We'd do North Wales on a subsequent trip. But we did get as far as Machynlleth and Dolgellau. In Machynlleth we stayed a night and visited the Center for Alternative Technology, a place where earth-friendly processes (solar and wind power systems, composting and mulching set ups, etc.) are on display for the public. The next day we drove up to Dolgellau where I made a video clip of me pronouncing the town's name (*Dolgethlie*) and emailed it to my father. I learned later that while he was able to download the image, he could not download the sound. Dolgelly lives on.

Our last day in Wales was spent cruising through the Foot-and-Mouth-smoke-filled Black Mountains, until we stumbled on the village of Llanthony Priory, where a 12th-century abbey offered, supposedly, cheap rooms. A nobleman had rebuilt one of the towers in the 18th century and now a couple of locals offer rooms for rent, some of which would get a big red

OSHA (Occupational Safety and Health Administration) stamp were they located on this side of the Atlantic. We picked the second highest room in the tower, and lugged our bags up, bumping our heads indiscriminately.

This is another amazing thing about Britain—the opportunities for bumping one's head on sharp stones. This all became a matter of concern back down south, in St. Davids, on the Pembrokeshire Peninsula. There, Ann, Zoe and I had visited the ruins of the medieval Bishops Palace, near St. Davids' famed cathedral. Wandering around the low-ceilinged rooms, I whacked my head numerous times on the sharp, 13th-century stones. More surprising than the amount of blood draining out of my head was the vast collection of signs warning of low roofs—signs I'd apparently missed. There were—and I'm not joking when I say it—about 18 variations on "Watch Your Head." Ann showed me all the signs as we were leaving. They were nailed to a rock wall near the entrance.

These signs depicted neat little white caricatures (on dark red backgrounds) smacking their skulls in every manner conceivable. Several signs showed the white caricatures falling down stairs and smashing the back sides of their craniums. A few depicted hunched, tired caricatures ascending stairs and gouging their foreheads to bits. Several more depicted caricatures holding their heads, as if the lingering headache was what would really count. This remarkable collection of signs was its own OSHA version of a gallery. Clearly, the management of Bishops Palace was prepared for non-English speakers.

Further, it seemed to me that the British race had evolved vertically since their ruins were built, and were now wandering around castles and abbeys with little space available for heads. In Llanthony Abbey, this became all the more apparent as we dined on Welsh lamb, washed down the meal with a few bitters, and proceeded to spike various parts of our skulls with exceedingly hard rocks. As far as I can tell, a typical British man is comparable to the typical European man anywhere—five to six feet in height, and anywhere from 130 to 190 pounds. If you wander around British abbeys, castles and old ruins from a few hundred years ago, however, you get the feeling these ancients were either dwarfs or hunchbacks, or hunchbacked dwarfs. Ann and I wished we'd brought helmets.

Yet Llanthony Abbey was enchanting for another reason—besides the intricately laid roof stones with their spots of blood and chunks of human head, we met some mystics. After dinner we met a fellow named Anthony, from South London, and his girlfriend Maureen, who were drinking beer in

the hotel lounge. They were clad in very traditional (i.e., Medieval) type garb, and apparently cruising along Britain's "lay lines," lines of energy that converge in certain places and draw mystics in droves. We struck up a conversation. They wanted to talk about American politics.

"It all seems a bit skew-iff, if you know what I mean," Anthony said in his thick cockney, in reference to Sen. John McCain's loss to George W. Bush in the 2000 Republican primary. "Wasn't he popular?"

I spent 20 minutes describing American politics and explaining that the United States is not, in fact, a democracy but a republic, and that politics here are like anywhere: a mix of big business, connections and ego. Might as well join a hunchbacked-dwarfs club and go spike your head in some old buildings.

Anyway, the night was rather pleasant, and after a solid sleep in the tower, we left the following morning. Anthony and Maureen, who'd slept in their van, greeted us as we departed, and gave Zoe a small white pebble.

"Hello darlin'. This here pebble's from Merlin's cave, down in Cornwall," Anthony explained. "Only a few people know where it is, and I'm one of the lucky few. It's good luck."

Zoe responded with her typical "aaargh" and attempted to eat the small rock. We bid adieu, and headed back toward England.

Wales is—simply put—lovely. It's a land that Anthony embodied, mystical, earthy, real. No pretense, but none is needed.

We drove through the lower Black Mountains, reminiscing of ages and characters past, and joined the A465 to Abergavenny, then the A4042 to Pontypool and Newport. Then, it was onto the M4 and across Southern England to London. I now drove with confidence, with an assured ability that would have made Merlin (and Anthony) proud, and the roundabouts fell by the way, armed soldiers who would do combat no more. We had beaten Britain's premier circular fantasy at its own game. We came, we saw, we enjoyed—and defeating the U.K. Highway Department in their game of "Spin the Motorist" was an unexpected sublime pleasure.

Maybe next time we'll even stop in at Laannnfinnagelcruckorny.

Notes about the Essays

"Maybe True. Maybe Not. Who cares?"
—Old saying of unknown origin

Although the many editors, readers and friends who have read some of these stories over the past few years have questioned the validity of the events and facts in these essays, all of the events and facts are, to the best of my knowledge, completely true.

These essays are, however, what most writers call "creative non-fiction," (a genre of writing that's currently taking a beating in some circles), stories that are true, but written in creative ways, sometimes with a little embellishment (sometimes with heaps). They relate a number of conversations and ideas that were obviously conjecture, but conjecture made while suffering in strange places and under strange circumstances.

For example, "Bathtubs Along the Ewaso Ngiro," is all completely true (even the attacking bee swarm), and was recorded because the reality of the situation was far more fascinating to me than any piece of conjecture or imaginative thinking. More specific notes on the publication of the stories follow.

East Africa

"The Shoes of Kilimanjaro," "Bathtubs Along the Ewaso Ngiro" and "I Dreamed of African Lions" were three short stories I wrote after coming back from a 1996 assignment to write a climbing guide, *Kilimanjaro & Mt. Kenya*. The book, a practical guide to the mountains, has now sold 15,000 copies.

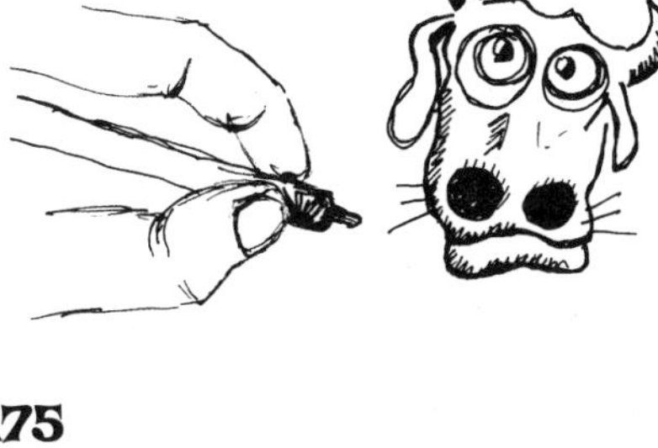

Anyway, my short story "The Shoes of Kilimanjaro," was a real surprise. Immediately after I wrote the story, it became the single most popular story in this collection and one of the most popular I have ever written. It was reprinted an astounding five times within a year, in magazines and adventure travel sections of newspapers all over the world.

While I like Hemingway's writing, I never thought his short story "The Snows of Kilimanjaro" was particularly great. I am astounded at how many times it has been reprinted over the years. Titling my story "The Shoes of Kilimanjaro," I aimed to create a saleable piece for magazines, but also to write a story that really is about Kilimanjaro. Hemingway's short story has only one reference to the mountain.

"The Shoes of Kilimanjaro" first appearance was in the Dispatches section of *The Aspen Times*, a newspaper to which I have contributed stories for the past ten years, as an adventure travel piece, in February 1998. It was subsequently published in a revised form in *Blue* magazine (New York), *Getaway* magazine (South Africa), *Vertical* magazine (Vail, Colorado), and *Rock & Ice* (Boulder, Colorado). In the fall of 2001, it appeared in a collection put together by *Walking* magazine, titled *The Walker Within* (the only essay not actually to have appeared in the magazine). During the winter of 2000–2001, it appeared in the Scottish magazine *TGO* (*The Great Outdoors*) and *Outdoor Australia*. It is scheduled to be reprinted in *I Should Have Just Stayed Home*, a forthcoming book to be published by RDR Books.

Likewise, "Bathtubs Along the Ewaso Ngiro" first appeared in *The Aspen Times*, as an adventure travel piece titled "Camel Safari," in July 1998. In 1999, it was reprinted in *Outpost*, a Canadian adventure travel magazine.

"I Dreamed of African Lions" was first published in *Tantravel*, a travel magazine in Dar Es Salaam, in the summer of 1998, in a completely different form. It was also printed in the adventure travel section of *Roaring Fork Sunday*, a now-defunct newspaper based in Basalt, Colorado, in September 1998.

Latin America

"Perro Café" first appeared in *The Aspen Times*, as an adventure travel piece, in June 1998. It was reprinted in *Discover Mexico* magazine (Markham, Ontario, Canada) in January 1999 (and I still have yet to be paid!), and in the 2001 book *I Really Should Have Stayed Home*, a collection of adventure travel stories published by RDR Books.

"In Patagonian Therapy" first appeared in *Climber* magazine (Sheffield, U.K.) in January 1997, and was reprinted in *Outdoor Australia* (Melbourne, Victoria) in the spring issue, 1997. In the summer of 1999, it was reprinted in the *Ascent* mountaineering journal (American Alpine Club Books, Denver, Colorado). In May 2000, it was reprinted in *Roaring Fork Sunday.*

"Touching the 'Roid" and "The Arachnids of Arenal" were first published in *Roaring Fork Sunday* in the winter of 2001 and spring of 1999, respectively, in different forms. In 2001, "Arachnids" was reprinted in *I Really Should Have Stayed Home*. "Inbreds in the Stream" also first appeared in *Roaring Fork Sunday*, in May 2000, in a very different form.

North America

"Dribbling Across the Elk Mountains: The Wilderness World Cup," was first published in *The Aspen Times* in early 1999, and was subsequently reprinted in *Apex* magazine. In 2001, it appeared in *I Really Should Have Stayed Home.*

Asia

Although I published five articles (to date) about a brief 1999 visit to India, "Holy Cows and Traffic Jams in India" was an amalgamation of all of them, and has never been published in this form.

"Out of the Box in Hong Kong" appeared in a slightly different form in *Roaring Fork Sunday* during winter 2001, and in a shorter version in *Outpost Magazine*. It is scheduled to be reprinted in *I Should Have Just Stayed Home*.

Australia

"The Sydney-to-Hobart Backwards," was first published in 1988, in a very different form, in *Outdoor Australia*. It was the first adventure story I had ever written, and I was amazed when, living a destitute life in my sister's garage in Sydney, I received a check for A$200.

Britain

"Round About Wales" first appeared in *The Aspen Times*, in the summer of 2001.

(The funding for these trips has been a combination of magazine and book assignments and advances, as well stories sold long after the trips. I have also regularly been "sponsored" by my trusty financial-backer, VISA card, who often lets me go months without paying him back. Two of these trips were travel-writer junkets—which, in the parlance, means free.)

About the Author

Travel writer Cameron M. Burns was born in Melbourne in 1965 and emigrated to the United States with his family in 1978. A Colorado-based writer, photographer, designer and communications specialist, Burns received a bachelor's degree in Environmental Design from the University of Colorado, with an emphasis on Architecture and Urban Design. After graduating, he worked as a movie technician in Hollywood before taking up writing, photography and design full-time. As a writer, he has authored or co-authored five climbing guidebooks, including *Kilimanjaro & Mt. Kenya*, *Colorado Ice Climber's Guide*, *California's Fourteeners: A Hiking & Climbing Guide*, *Climbing California's Fourteeners*, and *Selected Climbs of the Desert Southwest*. His essays have appeared in the books: *World Mountaineering* (U.K.), *Ascent*, *The Walker Within*, *I Really Should Have Stayed Home*, *I Should Have Just Stayed Home,* and *The Best of Rock & Ice*, as well as many other books and journals. As a photojournalist, Burns has been a staff correspondent/contributing editor for several dozen publications and has won seven awards for his writing and three for his photography. Much of his work has focused on environmental issues or outdoor activities, but he has also written hundreds of articles about politics, art, music and literature. He has shot assignments for *The* (London) *Times*, *Newsweek* and *GQ* magazine, among others. As an editor, Burns has maintained the U.S. bureau for several English magazines (*Mountain*, *Mountain Review)* and his popular column about mountaineering in North America—"Postcards from the Trailer Park"—appears in the British magazine *Climber*). He is currently finishing up *50 Hikes Colorado* (Countryman Press), with his one-year-old daughter and coauthor, Zoe.